THE PEAKS OF THE BALKANS TRAIL

THE PEAKS OF THE BALKANS TRAIL

MONTENEGRO, ALBANIA AND KOSOVO

by Rudolf Abraham

JUNIPER HOUSE, MURLEY MOSS,
OXENHOLME ROAD, KENDAL, CUMBRIA LA9 7RL
www.cicerone.co.uk

© Rudolf Abraham 2017
First edition 2017
ISBN: 978 1 85284 770 8
Reprinted 2019, 2023 (with updates)

Printed in India by Replika Press Pvt Ltd using responsibly sourced paper.
All photographs are by the author unless otherwise stated.
A catalogue record for this book is available from the British Library.

Route mapping by Lovell Johns www.lovelljohns.com
Contains OpenStreetMap.org data © OpenStreetMap
contributors, CC-BY-SA. NASA relief data courtesy of ESRI

For Tamara and Ivana

Updates to this guide

While every effort is made by our authors to ensure the accuracy of guide-books as they go to print, changes can occur during the lifetime of an edition. Any updates that we know of for this guide will be on the Cicerone website (www.cicerone.co.uk/770/updates), so please check before planning your trip. We also advise that you check information about such things as transport, accommodation and shops locally. Even rights of way can be altered over time.

The route maps in this guide are derived from publicly]available data, databases and crowd-sourced data. As such they have not been through the detailed checking procedures that would generally be applied to a published map from an official mapping agency, although naturally we have reviewed them closely in the light of local knowledge as part of the preparation of this guide.

We are always grateful for information about any discrepancies between a guidebook and the facts on the ground, sent by email to updates@cicerone.co.uk or by post to Cicerone, Juniper House, Murley Moss, Oxenholme Road, Kendal LA9 7RL, United Kingdom.

Register your book: To sign up to receive free updates, special offers and GPX files where available, create a Cicerone account and register your purchase via the 'My Account' tab at www.cicerone.co.uk.

Front cover: Maja Kolata from the 4WD road above Çeremi, Albania (Stage 3)

CONTENTS

Map key 7
Overview map 8
Route summary table 11

INTRODUCTION 13
Geography and geology 17
Historical summary 18
National parks and nature reserves 22
Wildlife and plants 22
Climate 27
When to hike 29
Getting there and around 30
Accommodation and food 35
Public holidays 36
Language 37
Money 38
Phones, internet and electricity 40
Cross-border permits 41
Local tour operators 43
Where to start/finish 44
Variations, transfers and highlights 46
Trail markings 48
Maps 49
Equipment 50
Water 52
Safety in the mountains and what to do in an emergency 54
Using this guide 59

THE PEAKS OF THE BALKANS TRAIL 61
Stage 1   Theth (Albania) – Valbona (Albania) 62
Stage 2   Valbona (Albania) – Çeremi (Albania) via the Prosllopit Pass 69
Stage 3   Çeremi (Albania) – Dobërdol (Albania) 77
Stage 4   Dobërdol (Albania) – Milishevc (Kosovo) 83
Stage 5   Milishevc (Kosovo) – Rekë e Allagës (Kosovo) 89
Stage 6   Rekë e Allagës (Kosovo) – Drelaj or Restaurant Te Liqeni (Kosovo) . 94
Stage 7   Restaurant Te Liqeni (Kosovo) – Babino polje (Montenegro) 101

Stage 8   Babino polje (Montenegro) – Plav (Montenegro) 107
Stage 9   Plav (Montenegro) – Vusanje (Montenegro) 114
Stage 10   Vusanje (Montenegro) – Theth (Albania) 120

Appendix A   Useful contacts. 129
Appendix B   Accommodation. 132
Appendix C   Further reading. 136
Appendix D   Language and glossary 138
Appendix E   History timeline 149

Acknowledgements

First and foremost I would like to thank Endrit Shima and Ricardo Fahrig at Zbulo and Vlatko Bulatović at Zalaz for all their help, support and enthusiasm during the time I researched and wrote this guide, for which I am extremely grateful. It's people like you who help make this such an amazing part of the world to visit, so a very sincere *faleminderit shumë* and *mnogo vam hvala* to all three of you. Thanks are also due to Ahmet Reković in Plav, Pavlin Polia and family in Theth, Vucija Martić in Plav, Armend Alija and family in Babino polje, Montor Bojku in Pejë, Emma and Ben Heywood in Virpazar, Hayley Wright in Herceg Novi, and Nicky Brown at Black Sheep and Germania for generously providing flights to Pristina on my last trip to Prokletije. And to my wife Ivana, with whom I first fell in love with Prokletije in the early noughties.

Symbols used on route maps

~	route
~ - ~	alternative route
~	connecting route
(S) (F)	start point/finish point
~ - ~	track
~	4x4 vehicle track
~	tarmac road
	woodland
	urban areas
	international border
~ ~	disputed border
▲	peak
⌂	katun (shepherd's hut/ summer settlement)
🍴	restaurant
☕	café/bar (drinks only)
🏠	hotel/guesthouse
■	building
☦ † ☪	church/cemetery/mosque
©	cave
)(	pass
• (W)	water feature/spring
🚌	bus stop
⚊	campsite

Relief in metres
5000 and above
4800–5000
4600–4800
4400–4600
4200–4400
4000–4200
3800–4000
3600–3800
3400–3600
3200–3400
3000–3200
2800–3000
2600–2800
2400–2600
2200–2400
2000–2200
1800–2000
1600–1800
1400–1600
1200–1400
1000–1200
800–1000
600–800
400–600
200–400
0–200

SCALE: 1:50,000

0 kilometres 0.5   1

0 miles   0.5

Contour lines are drawn at 25m intervals and highlighted at 100m intervals.

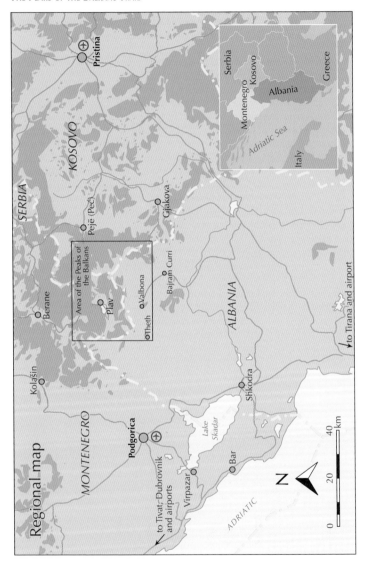

Regional map

Early morning view from Bajrak, a 2047m peak above Lake Plav, on the trail to Vusanje (Stage 9)

On the saddle above Liqeni i Kuçishtës, Kosovo (Stage 7)

ROUTE SUMMARY TABLE

Stage	Start	Finish	Distance	Ascent/Descent	Time	Page
1	Theth (Albania)	Valbona (Albania)	19.5km	1070m/850m	8hrs	62
2	Valbona (Albania)	Çeremi (Albania)	14km or 11km	1200m/950m or 540m/380m	7hrs 30mins or 4hrs 30mins	69
3	Çeremi (Albania)	Dobërdol (Albania)	15.5km	1030m/440m	7hrs	77
4	Dobërdol (Albania)	Milishevc (Kosovo)	23km	1440m/1500m	8hrs	83
5	Milishevc (Kosovo)	Rekë e Allagës (Kosovo)	16km	860m/1270m	6hrs	89
6	Rekë e Allagës (Kosovo)	Drelaj or Restaurant Te Liqeni (Kosovo)	10km or 23km	530m/710m or 1260m/1140m	3hrs 45mins or 7hrs 30mins	94
7	Restaurant Te Liqeni (Kosovo)	Babino polje (Montenegro)	16km	1150m/1110m	7hrs 30mins	101
8	Babino polje (Montenegro)	Plav (Montenegro)	20km	720m/1250m	6hrs 30mins	107
9	Plav (Montenegro)	Vusanje (Montenegro)	27.5km	1140m/1080m	8hrs	114
10	Vusanje (Montenegro)	Theth (Albania)	21.3km	1110m/1440m	7hrs 30mins	120
Total	Theth (Albania)	Theth (Albania)	182.8km	10250m	69hrs 45mins	

Maja e Boshit (Maja Bošit), a prominent 2416m peak southeast of the Valbona Pass (Stage 1)

INTRODUCTION

Descending to Vusanje and the Ropojana Valley (Stage 9)

The Peaks of the Balkans is a recently developed cross-border long-distance trail through the spectacularly wild and rugged borderlands of Montenegro, Albania and Kosovo. A circular route of around 192km in length, it takes in remote valleys, lakes and mountain passes, winding its way through some stupendous mountain scenery and passing through traditional mountain villages which often feel like somewhere time forgot. It's a corner of Europe few people are familiar with, let alone visit. Food and accommodation are offered in traditional village home stays, so there's no need to carry camping gear, with delicious regional cuisine and genuine hospitality that is frankly a million

miles away from some of the more lacklustre tourist resorts on the coast. The route can be hiked in around 10 days or stretched out over a couple of weeks, with about a third of the whole trek lying in each country.

The bulk of the mountain scenery on the Peaks of the Balkans Trail is provided by the Prokletije mountains (Bjeshkët e Nemuna in Albanian), whose name translates rather charmingly as 'the accursed mountains' – created, according to local folklore, by the devil himself, unleashed from hell for a single day of mischief. The biodiversity of the region is extraordinary. The Montenegrin side of Prokletije was recently designated a national park – the newest and still the least visited of Montenegro's five national parks, a great glacier-scoured area (the glaciers themselves are long gone) bristling with spiky mountain peaks boasting suitably evocative names like Očnjak ('Fang') and Koplje ('Spear'). There are two more national parks on the Albanian side, and another in Kosovo.

The trail was developed by the German development corporation GIZ in conjunction with national and local tourism organisations and hiking clubs, in order to create a sustainable income for the local population in these mountainous areas of Albania, Kosovo and Montenegro, to encourage sustainable local tourism and to bring these parts of the region closer together across political borders. Despite increasing visitor numbers – largely due to the growing popularity of the Peaks of the Balkans trail – the area remains incredibly underdeveloped and unspoilt, much of it having been off limits to foreigners until comparatively recently. This is the first English-language guidebook to hiking the Peaks of the Balkans.

Since it's a circular route, there are several points at which you can choose to start and finish hiking the Trail (the various merits of which are described in 'Where to start/finish') – and there are two points where the 'circuit' meets, like a figure of eight. Starting from the village of Theth in Albania, the route crosses a pass to

Katun Treskavička, on a hillside between Babino polje and Plav in Montenegro (Stage 8)

reach the Valbona Valley, and climbs to the Montenegrin border below Maja Kolata, one of the highest peaks in the area, before descending to the tiny settlement of Çeremi. Later it passes through the remote summer settlement of Dobërdol before crossing the border into Kosovo, and descends to the Rugova Gorge. Crossing into Montenegro it passes through Babino polje then climbs to Lake Hrid, before descending to the town of Plav and, after crossing Vrh Bora, to the village of Vusanje, before following the Ropojana valley up into Albania again, crossing the Pëjë Pass and descending to Theth.

The trail is well marked for much of its length, a reasonably good map is available covering the whole route, and access is relatively straightforward – sometimes extremely straightforward – to several points along the way by local buses. Good, knowledgeable local guides are available to accompany groups or individuals along the route. Hiking is along existing paths and 4WD tracks and is not technically difficult – however the surrounding mountains are high and the weather can change suddenly and dramatically, and for the most part the route is very remote. Exit points, should you need to break your trek short in an emergency, may be several days apart, and may not be in the country you arrived in.

It's possible to start and finish the Peaks of the Balkans in any of the three countries through which it

passes, however whichever starting point you decide on, you'll need to obtain a cross-border permit from the relevant authorities in Montenegro, Albania or Kosovo before setting off and actually walking the trail. Judging by the helpful and informative Peaks of the Balkans website (www.peaksoftheballkans.com), you would be forgiven for thinking this should be easy enough to do yourself, but in fact it's not quite as straightforward as you might expect, and it is worth simply getting a local agency to sort out the permit. See 'Cross-border permits' below for further guidance.

I first visited the Prokletije mountains back in 2004, staying a few days in a mountain hut in the Grbaja Valley in Montenegro. One day I walked along the Ropojana Valley – a broad ribbon of green framed by limestone peaks, their tops festooned with clouds – towards a lonely lake on the border with Albania. The Peaks of the Balkans wasn't yet born at that time, the Montenegrin part of Prokletije had not yet been declared a national park, and the only people we encountered on these well-marked trails through some of the most beautiful mountain scenery anywhere in Europe were a handful of Albanian children gathering wild strawberries. It all seemed fantastically, almost unbelievably remote and unspoilt. Returning to Prokletije in 2016 to research and write this guide, I was pleased to find that feeling of isolation little changed.

Key facts and figures

Montenegro

Country name	Montenegro (Crna gora)
Capital	Podgorica
Language	Montenegrin (Serbian)
Currency	Euro
Population	625,266 (2011 census)
Land surface area	14,026km²
Time zone	GMT +1 (CET)
International telephone code	+383
Electricity	220V/50Hz

Albania

Country name	Republic of Albania (Albanian: Shqipëri; Gheg dialect: Shqipni)
Capital	Tirana (alternative spelling: Tiranë)
Language	Albanian
Currency	Lek
Population	2.8 million (2011 census)
Land surface area	28,748km²
Time zone	GMT +1 (CET)
International telephone code	+355
Electricity	220V/50Hz

Kosovo

Country name	Republic of Kosovo (Albanian: Kosova)
Capital	Pristina (alternative spellings: Prishtina, Priština)
Languages	Albanian and Serbian
Currency	Euro
Population	1.9 million (estimate)
Land surface area	10,908km²
Time zone	GMT +1 (CET)
International telephone code	+383
Electricity	220V/50Hz

Krš Bogićevica, viewed from the pass above Dobërdol, on the border between Albania and Montenegro (Stage 4)

GEOGRAPHY AND GEOLOGY

The mountains through which the Peaks of the Balkans route passes form the border between Albania, Montenegro and Kosovo. They occupy an area south of the River Lim and north of the Black Drin, bordered to the west and east by Lake Skadar and the headwaters of the White Drin respectively.

Collectively, these mountains are known by several names – Prokletije or Bjeshkët e Namuna, meaning the 'accursed mountains', in Montenegrin and Albanian respectively, or (the part lying in Albania) the Albanian Alps. In some places, you may see signs referring to them as the 'blessed mountains' – a nice attempt to challenge the negative connotations of the 'accursed' part of their name (and frankly, when you're hiking through this astonishingly beautiful part of Europe, this does seem more appropriate). In any case, for convenience, we'll refer to them as Prokletije here. Prokletije forms the south part of the Dinaric Alps, a chain of mountains stretching some 700km and running in a northwest to southeast direction from the Slovenian border through Croatia, Bosnia, Montenegro, Albania and Kosovo.

The Prokletije mountains are characterised by broad, glaciated valleys and steep-sided limestone peaks, particularly in the western half of the range in Albania and Montenegro – in Kosovo, the eastern half of the range has a more gentle profile. They include the highest peak in Montenegro (Maja Kolata, 2528m) and the highest peak in Kosovo (Gjeravica, 2656m), as well as the highest mountain in the

17

Dinaric Alps, Maja Jezerces (2694m) in Albania (the highest mountain in Albania is Korab, 2764m, which lies further southeast on the border with Macedonia). All three of these can be climbed with only slight detours from the Peaks of the Balkans Trail, as can several other prominent peaks.

The Prokletije mountains were formed some 100 million years ago, during the same period and process as the Alps – through the buckling and uplifting/folding of the Eurasian plate with the African plate, and the uplifting of the what had once been the bed of a shallow, tropical sea, where shells and other marine life had been deposited in layers over millions of years. The area is heavily glaciated (although no glaciers remain here today), and glaciation occurred at a lower altitude than in the Alps further north – Lake Plav is the largest glacial lake in the Balkans, and a glacier in the Plav/Gusinje area is thought to have been around 35km long and up to 200m thick.

Karst features – distinctive fluting, pans, sinkholes and limestone pavement formed by the gradual dissolving of limestone rock by rainwater – are prominent in Prokletije, particularly in the western half of the range. However, unlike most other popular hiking areas in the karst mountains of Montenegro (and neighbouring Croatia), availability of surface water is good on the Peaks of the Balkans Trail, with fairly abundant springs and mountain streams.

HISTORICAL SUMMARY

For a more detailed historical timeline, see Appendix E.

Rocky trail with karst features near the Prosllopit Pass, Montenegro (Stage 2)

Early times
The history of the mountainous borderlands between Albania, Kosovo and Montenegro – along with much of the Balkans – is long, complex and incredibly rich. Unfortunately however, it is little known or understood in western Europe beyond the prism of recent civil war, conflict and political turmoil.

By the first millennium BC Bronze Age tribes – collectively known as the Illyrians – were established along the eastern Adriatic seaboard (including Montenegro and Albania) and further inland, while Corinthian colonists founded trading cities along the coast and islands. The Romans began their gradual conquest of the Illyrians from the third century BC, leading to the creation of the Roman province of Illyricum (later renamed Dalmatia) which roughly included modern Croatia, Montenegro and Albania, and further inland, the province of Moesia which included modern Serbia and Kosovo. The Romans built roads and cities, developed trade and exploited the area's wealth of natural resources including minerals (for which eastern Kosovo was particularly important) and wood. Both Albania and Montenegro still have impressive Roman remains, including UNESCO-listed Butrint in Albania.

The Illyrians didn't simply vanish – several Roman emperors including Aurelius and Diocletian were actually of Illyrian descent, and a number of Illyrian tribes also left their names in the region, including the words *Dalmatia* (from the Delmatae tribe) and *Adriatic* (from the Ardiaei).

Following the collapse of the Roman Empire in the fourth century AD, and a succession of Hunnish and Gothic invasions, Slavic tribes settled in the Balkans from the sixth century AD. Byzantium remained a dominant influence in the Balkans, albeit waxing and waning with the rise and fall of other powers in the region such as the Bulgars.

The medieval period
During the 11th century the Serbian state of Duklja (in what is now Montenegro) gained independence

Wooden minaret in snowfall, Plav (Stage 8)

19

from Byzantium, while the following century in Albania, Arbanon was established as a semi-autonomous principality. Duklja was in turn absorbed into Raška, which grew into medieval Serbia, and by the 14th century Montenegro, Albania and Kosovo were all incorporated into the vast medieval Serbian Empire. The seat of the Serbian Patriarchate (Orthodox Church) was located in Peć (Pejë), in Kosovo, and the medieval architecture of Peć and Deçan – just east of the Peaks of the Balkans Trail, and a very worthy detour – is a UNESCO World Heritage Site.

With the defeat of Serbian and other Christian armies by the Ottomans at the Battle of Kosovo in 1389, Albania, Kosovo and Montenegro all fell under Ottoman rule for some 500 years. In Albania in particular, the following centuries saw a widespread conversion to Islam. Meanwhile Venice annexed most of the southern Adriatic coast, including the Albanian and Montenegrin coasts – a hold it would maintain until Napoleon Bonaparte extinguished the Venetian Republic in 1797.

Early 20th century

Serbia and Montenegro, together with Greece and Bulgaria, successfully attacked and defeated the Ottomans during the First Balkan War in 1912, leading to the Ottomans ceding most of their territories in the Balkans. Serbia regained Kosovo, Albania declared its independence. However at the end of the First World War, Montenegro became the only Allied country to lose its independence, becoming instead a part of Serbia when the Kingdom of Serbs, Croats and Slovenes was proclaimed in 1918.

During the Second World War the Kingdom of Yugoslavia was invaded by Hitler's Germany, Albania by Mussolini and later Germany. In 1945, Montenegro – along with Serbia, Croatia, Bosnia, Slovenia and Macedonia (Kosovo had the status of an autonomous province within Serbia) – became a state within the Federal Republic of Yugoslavia, under Tito. Meanwhile in Albania, the head of the new Communist Party Enver Hoxha became ruler. Tito formally broke ranks with Stalinism in 1948, while Hoxha followed a more isolationist policy, and later turned increasingly towards Communist China.

Recent conflicts

Following the death of Tito in 1980, Serbian leader Slobodan Milošević rose to power in Yugoslavia, fanning nationalist sentiment and reducing the autonomous status of Kosovo within Yugoslavia. Croatia declared its independence from Serbia following a referendum in 1991, and during the ensuing war between Serbia and Croatia (Croatian War of Independence), Montenegro allied itself with Serbia. Following this conflict, Serbia and Montenegro maintained the name Yugoslavia, but from

2002 this confederation was renamed the State Union of Serbia and Montenegro. Calls by the Albanian majority in Kosovo for greater autonomy within Yugoslavia led to the Kosovo War in the late 1990s, between Yugoslav forces and the Kosovo Liberation Army, prompting a huge exodus of refugees into Albania, and Nato airstrikes on Serbia.

Kosovo declared its independence from Serbia in 2008, the declaration being recognised by most EU states as well as by Montenegro – which has distanced itself from Serbia's stance on Kosovo – but not by Serbia, which still views this area as the cradle of medieval Serbia. A large stretch of the border between Montenegro and Kosovo remains disputed, and a drive from Berane in Montenegro to Peć in Kosovo goes through around 7km of remote and spectacularly beautiful no-man's-land.

In 1990, the Communist regime in Albania allowed the formation of independent political parties for the first time. However the country descended into anarchy in the late 1990s following the collapse of fraudulent pyramid investment schemes, through which many Albanians saw their life's savings vanish.

21st century

In May 2006 Montenegro held a referendum and voted by a narrow margin for independence from Serbia. Although the EU began accession talks with Montenegro in 2012, at the time of writing (2017) any potential prospect of EU membership remains several years away. Both Montenegro and Albania are members of Nato.

The church in Theth, Albania, built in 1892 (Stage 10)

NATIONAL PARKS AND NATURE RESERVES

Prokletije National Park, in Montenegro, covers an area of 16,630ha. It is the newest of Montenegro's five national parks, having been designated as such in 2009 – a strikingly beautiful mountain landscape, the fauna and in particular the flora of which are fantastically rich. Within Prokletije National Park, the area around Hridsko jezero is a nature reserve (Rezervat prirodne Hridsko jezero), as is Volušnica in the Grbaja Valley.

The Peaks of the Balkans Trail passes through two national parks in Albania: Thethi National Park and Valbona Valley National Park. Thethi National Park covers an area of 2630ha in the Thethi Valley, and was declared a national park in 1966. The Valbona Valley National Park covers an area of 8000ha, and was declared a national park in 1996.

The Rugova Valley and surrounding mountains in Kosovo were declared a national park in 2013, covering an area of 20,330ha. There is some opposition to the new park from some locals, who fear it will affect their ability to collect firewood and graze livestock in the area, or to build houses there.

Despite the presence of these national parks, the area is not without its own environmental issues. In the Valbona Valley, there are proposals for a large number of hydroelectric power plants, some of them within the protected area of the national park itself. Pollution of mountain rivers from toilets – in some cases built directly above streams, as at Dobërdol – is another concern, in particular given the sharp (and continuing) increase of trekkers on the Peaks of the Balkans Trail.

WILDLIFE AND PLANTS

The biodiversity of the Prokletije mountains in Albania, Kosovo and

VALBONA RIVER HYDROELECTRIC POWER PLANTS

There are plans to construct no fewer than 14 hydroelectric power plants along a 30km stretch of the Valbona River, with eight of these to be within the Valbona National Park itself. Despite local residents having filed numerous official complaints, and concerns having been raised by national and international organisations including EuroNatur and the WWF, there has been little or no response to these objections from the Albanian government: they simply argue that the concessions for the projects were made by the previous government, and imply they are unable or unwilling to stop them going ahead – even though they admit they should never have been granted.

View on the approach to the Valbona Pass (Stage 1)

Catherine Bohne and Alfred Selimaje, who run the Rilindja Guesthouse in Valbona, are doing what they can to raise awareness of these proposals, which would obviously have a catastrophic impact on the environment and surrounding landscape – which is simultaneously the region's main draw card for tourism and the basis for a sustainable local economy. Local residents, represented by an NGO, TOKA, have moved to block the projects by filing a lawsuit against the government. Nevertheless, in September 2016 bulldozers moved into position in the Dragobi and Maskollata regions of Valbona National Park.

You can find out more about the proposed hydroelectric projects in the Valbona Valley at www.toka-albania.org.

Montenegro is extraordinary, from large carnivores to raptors to clouds of butterflies, and one of the most spectacularly rich flora of anywhere in Europe.

Mammals

Prokletije is home to small numbers of Europe's three large carnivore species – brown bear, grey wolf and Eurasian lynx – with their distribution limited in all cases to the remotest areas of the range. Crucial to the survival of these iconic species in the region is maintaining effective wildlife corridors – the so-called Balkan Green Belt along the border areas of Montenegro, Albania and Kosovo as well as between Albania and Macedonia (part of the European Green Belt initiative) which EuroNatur (www.euronatur.org) has been working to protect and strengthen since 2004.

Man on a donkey near the Pejë Pass, Albania (Stage 10)

Encounters between humans and bears are very rare; in more than 15 years of hiking in the Balkans the author has never seen more than a few paw prints in the snow, and some scat.

The Eurasian lynx survives in small numbers in Prokletije. A critically endangered subspecies of the Eurasian lynx, the Balkan lynx, survives in very small numbers in Prokletije and in the border area between Albania and Macedonia – there are thought to be as few as just 35 individuals left, making it one of the rarest cats on earth.

Other more common mammals include wild boar, roe deer, chamois, fox, pine marten, common dormouse and Alpine shrew. Bat species inhabiting the caves of Prokletije include the Mediterranean horseshoe bat, Geoffrey's bat, greater mouse-eared

bat and others. The Eurasian otter, categorized as near-threatened on the IUCN Red List, is also present.

Reptiles and amphibians

Several species of snake inhabit the Prokletije mountains, two of them venomous. These are the nose-horned viper, known locally as *poskok* or *nëpërka me bri* in Montenegrin/Albanian respectively; and the common viper or adder, known locally as *šarka* or *nëpërka e malit*. The nose-horned viper is the more venomous of the two (it's Europe's most venomous snake), and also the more aggressive; it is either light grey or brownish copper, with a dark black zigzag pattern along its back, and is easily recognizable by the prominent soft horn at the end of its snout. The common viper is generally around 55cm, with a zigzag pattern along the back. (It is worth mentioning that both the nose-horned viper and the common viper also occur in other, more frequently visited parts of Europe – for example, the former is found in northern Italy, while the latter is Europe's most widespread venomous snake, and is found in the UK.) Other species of snake include the large whip snake, Balkan whip snake, Dahl's whip snake, Montpellier snake, grass snake, dice snake and the tiny worm snake.

Snakes are very unlikely to strike except in self-defence (for example, if you step on them), and walking boots and hiking poles will usually alert a snake of your approach and give it time to slither off. See 'Safety in the mountains and what to do in an emergency' for more information.

A number of lizards are common in Prokletije, including the Balkan green lizard (which grows up to 16cm or more in length), green lizard, Balkan wall lizard, Dalmatian algyroides (unmistakable, with its striking, blue-coloured throat), slow worm and Prokletije rock lizard – the latter a species endemic to Prokletije and known only from a few isolated locations.

The amphibian you'll probably see most commonly hiking the Peaks of the Balkans Trail is the fire salamander, easily recognised by its bright yellow spots. Other species found in Prokletije include Alpine newt, Balkan crested newt, Balkan stream frog, Albanian water frog and yellow-bellied toad.

A useful resource for identifying the reptiles and amphibians of Europe is www.herp.it.

Birds

Prokletije is very rich in birdlife, with high mountain areas particularly

Fire salamander (Salamandra salamandra) on a trail near Plav

25

important for breeding raptors and Lake Plav providing a significant area for waterfowl and migratory species. Some 161 different species of bird have been recorded in Prokletije National Park (Montenegro) and 179 species recorded in Kosovo.

Raptors to look out for in the mountains include the golden eagle – a huge bird, fairly easy to identify by its long wings, long tail and sheer size – the short-toed snake eagle, Bonelli's eagle, griffon vulture, common buzzard, goshawk, peregrine falcon and European honey buzzard. The latter is more closely related to a kite than to the common buzzard, and has an extraordinarily wide colour variation – generally in imitation of other birds of prey inhabiting the same area.

Prokletije is a particularly good area for rock partridge, and you also have a chance of seeing the Eurasian eagle-owl – one of the largest species of owl, with huge ear tufts – Eurasian scops-owl, hazel grouse, red-backed shrike, yellow-billed chough, Alpine chough, wallcreeper, ring ouzel, white-winged snowfinch, Alpine accentor, horned Lark, European nightjar, rock nuthatch and common crossbill. Several species of woodpecker are present, including the lesser-spotted woodpecker, grey-headed woodpecker and the endangered three-toed woodpecker.

On or around lake Plav, look for grey heron, great crested grebe, black-necked grebe, little grebe, great bittern and corncrake. The lake is home to the largest breeding population of corncrake in Montenegro.

Journey to Valbona have prepared a very useful checklist of birds in the Valbona Valley, based on information from the Albanian Ornithologist Dr Taulant Bino, which can be downloaded from www.journeytovalbona.com (select 'About', then 'Birds').

Butterflies

The Prokletije mountains are incredibly rich in butterflies, with 130 species having been recorded in Prokletije National Park in Montenegro alone, and 129 species recorded the area of Prokletije in Kosovo (to put these figures in context, there are just 67 species of butterfly in the UK!). Butterfly species recorded along the Peaks of the Balkans Trail include common swallowtail, scarce swallowtail, twin-spot fritillary, lesser-spotted fritillary, small tortoiseshell, mountain apollo and several species of blue including northern blue, turquoise blue and mazarine blue.

Plants

The Balkan peninsula constitutes one of the richest plant areas in Europe, with an estimated 7000 or more species of plants – a figure which includes numerous endemics and, because the region was not under permanent ice caps during the glacial periods of the Quaternary era, a number of Tertiary relics (species that were more widely distributed during the Tertiary Period).

Orchid beside the path from Çeremi to Dobërdol (Stage 3); bellflower (Campanula) near the Zavoj pass, Montenegro (Stage 7)

Around 2000 species of plant have been recorded in Prokletije National Park in Montenegro, of which some 225 species are endemic. At least 1650 plant species were recorded in Theth National Park in Albania, 85 of which are rare or threatened, and four endemic; and over 1500 plant species in the area of Prokletije located in Kosovo.

Along the lower sections of the Peaks of the Balkans Trail, coniferous, mixed and broadleaved forests dominate: Aleppo pine, Norwegian spruce, beech, mountain maple, white oak and to a lesser extent the regionally endemic Macedonian pine and Bosnian pine. At higher altitudes these are replaced by Alpine vegetation including mountain pine and juniper.

Rich sub-alpine pastures and grasslands or areas of scrub extend above the tree line, giving way to bare rock and scree.

Wild thyme and other herbs carpet the ground in places, and blueberries grow in profusion during the summer months, along with blackberries and wild strawberries – hiking at this time is sometimes reduced to a slow but very enjoyable grazing pace. The number of fungi is astonishing; there are an estimated 2000 or so species in Montenegro alone.

CLIMATE

The Prokletije mountains experience moderate summers and long, harsh winters. Daytime temperatures during the summer are warm but not unpleasantly so, reaching up to around 25°C in July/August, the nights refreshingly cool. July is the driest month of the year in Prokletije, followed by August and June, although the weather here is notoriously fickle and you shouldn't rule out the possibility of showers, even in the summer months.

Over 90% of precipitation occurs during the winter, with precipitation generally at its highest in November. Winters in Prokletije are long and harsh, with heavy snowfall (between one and three metres). The first snowfall in the mountains is usually sometime in October, and is at its heaviest in November/December, with snow lingering well into the summer months, particularly on northern slopes. The snowline in Prokletije is considerably lower than in the Alps – around 1500m.

In general, northerly winds are colder and drier, bringing more stable, clear weather conditions during the summer, and snow in the winter; southerly winds tend to bring warm, moist air, leading to rain during the summer and snowfall during the winter. As in other parts of the Dinaric Alps, the northerly wind (called the *bura*) can be quite strong, with gusts reaching gale force.

The Montenegrin and Albanian coasts and lowlands enjoy long, hot summers and short, mild winters. In Montenegro's Zeta plain, summer months can be oppressively hot – the Montenegrin capital, Podgorica, had the highest summer maximum temperatures recorded in the former Yugoslavia, while Orjen, above the north end of the Montenegrin coast, has one of the highest annual rainfalls recorded anywhere in Europe.

Plav, Montenegro (958m)					
Month	Jan	Feb	Mar	Apr	May
mm rainfall	111	99	97	99	101
°C (mean)	-1.4	0.3	4.1	7.8	12.4
°C (min)	-4.6	-3.4	-0.1	3.2	7.4
°C (max)	1.9	4	8.4	12.4	17.4
Theth, Albania (963m)					
Month	Jan	Feb	Mar	Apr	May
mm rainfall	125	112	107	107	101
°C (mean)	-0.8	0.7	4.1	7.8	12.4
°C (min)	-4	-2.9	0	3.3	7.5
°C (max)	2.5	4.3	8.3	12.3	17.4

Alpine shelter near Hridsko jezero (Stage 8)

WHEN TO HIKE

The hiking season on the Peaks of the Balkans Trail begins in May or June, with the latter bringing more settled weather and milder temperatures – although you can still expect snow patches in June, or until July in higher areas. Wildflowers are at their most

June	July	Aug	Sept	Oct	Nov	Dec
79	66	68	90	110	139	128
15.7	18.1	18.0	14.6	9.9	4.3	0.3
10.7	12.6	12.4	9.3	5.4	0.9	-2.7
20.8	23.6	23.7	20.0	14.4	7.7	3.4

June	July	Aug	Sept	Oct	Nov	Dec
77	62	67	95	120	155	143
15.9	18.3	18.3	14.8	10.2	4.8	1
10.9	12.8	12.7	9.6	5.8	1.4	-2.0
20.9	23.8	23.9	20.1	14.6	8.3	4.1

spectacular in June. July is statistically the driest month, followed by August and June – but this doesn't mean you shouldn't be prepared for possible rain or thunderstorms during these months, just as at any other time of year. August is the hottest month. By September snowfields have dried up, and with them possibly some springs; nights will be getting cooler and you can expect frost. In October the landscape turns to beautiful autumn colours, and the first snowfall arrives sometime this month, which generally marks the end of the trekking season in Prokletije.

GETTING THERE AND AROUND

Since the Peaks of the Balkans Trail is a circular route, it is possible to start or finish the route in Montenegro, Kosovo or Albania – meaning a flight to Podgorica, Pristina or Tirana, and continuing to a trailhead by local bus

from there. On balance, at least if arriving from the UK, cheaper flights and more direct onward transport to the Trail favour flying to Podgorica or Pristina. (See later in this section for advantages/disadvantages of the different possible places to start/finish hiking the Trail.) See Appendix A for a list of useful contacts.

Visas

UK passport holders can enter Albania, Kosovo and Montenegro as a tourist without a visa and stay for a period of 90 days, as can most EU passport holders including Dutch, French and German nationals. Similarly, US, Canadian and Australian passport holders do not need a visa to enter Montenegro, Albania or Kosovo as a tourist, and can stay for up to 90 days. Other passport holders should check visa requirements through the Ministry of Foreign Affairs of each of

Katun Bajrović, a summer settlement above Babino polje, Montenegro (Stage 8)

the three countries through which the Peaks of the Balkans Trail passes:

- Ministry of Foreign Affairs, Albania: www.punetejashtme. gov.al
- Ministry of Foreign Affairs, Kosovo: www.mfa-ks.net
- Ministry of Foreign Affairs and European Integration, Montenegro: www.mvpei.gov.me

(Select the English-language option and look for consular services/affairs.)

The above three websites are also the place to find the addresses and contact details of foreign diplomatic missions (ie consulates and embassies) in Albania, Kosovo and Montenegro. Make a note of these before you travel.

Note however that the Peaks of the Balkans Trail is in a sensitive border area and you must obtain a cross-border permit before hiking the route (see 'Cross-border permits').

Flights to Podgorica (Montenegro)

Ryanair (www.ryanair.com) fly direct from the UK to the Montenegrin capital, Podgorica, three times a week. From Podgorica you can either continue by bus to Plav (in Montenegro) and start hiking from there, or continue by bus and ferry via Skhodër to Theth or Valbona (both in Albania), and begin your trek there.

Podgorica

Podgorica Airport (https://montenegroairports.com/), called Golubovci) is around 15km south of the Montenegrin capital. There's no airport shuttle bus, so it's best to get a taxi (tel +382 (0)69 949 197; www.taxi-travel.me) to Podgorica bus station or your hotel, which shouldn't cost more than €10–€15. (You can get a local bus on the Podgorica–Bar route, but you need to walk from the airport terminal down to the main road and flag down the bus there – and there's no guarantee it will stop if already full.)

The main bus station (Trg Goolootočkih žrtava 1, Podgorica; tel +382 (0)20 620 430; https://busticket4.me/EN) is a 15min walk southeast from the downtown area and Trg Republika, across the River Morača, or a 10min walk southeast from the old clock tower (Sahat Kula) and the old town.

If you're planning, or need, to stop in Podgorica for a night or more at the start or end of your trek, Hotel Terminus is good, clean and better value than most accommodation in the Montenegrin capital, and is located right next to the bus station (www.booking.com/hotel/me/terminus-hotel-podgorica.en-gb.html). Pod Volat (Trg Vojvode Bećir Bega Osmanagića, Podgorica) is a good-value restaurant serving a wide range of local dishes, next to the old clock tower (Sahat Kula) – a 10min walk northwest from the bus station.

Podgorica airport is actually almost as close to Lake Skadar National Park as it is to Podgorica, so staying in Virpazar (from where there are buses to Podgorica) is another possibility, with some kayaking or a wine tour thrown in for good measure – contact Undiscovered Montenegro for accommodation in Virpazar or tours in the Lake Skadar region (www.undiscoveredmontenegro.com).

Podgorica to Plav

Around five buses a day make the 4hr journey from Podgorica bus station to Plav. Buses do sometimes fill up, so it's worth buying your ticket as soon as you get to the bus station. Bus times from Podgorica can be found at https://busticket4.me/EN.

Podgorica to Theth or Valbona

By public transport, this is a less direct route than Podgorica–Plav. There are two buses a day from Podgorica to Skhodër in Albania (journey time 90mins, timetables at www.buster minal.me/timetable), from where you can take another bus along the steep road to Theth (journey time 2hrs 30mins, usually departing early in the morning). Alternatively – and more scenically – take a bus from Skhodër to Koman (2hrs), from where you can take the ferry across Lake Koman, following the flooded course of the River Drin (timetables at https://koma-nilakeferry.com/en/)) – this ferry ride being the main reason for following this route. Of the two ferry operators, Berisha and Mario Molla, the latter offers the advantage of including ferry

View across Lake Plav towards the mouth of the Ropojana Valley (Stage 8)

and connecting minibus services in one single booking. Otherwise, from Fierze where the ferry arrives at the north end of the lake, take a minibus to Bajram Curri (minibuses meet the ferry, as do taxis so make sure you know which one you're getting by asking the fare); and from there, a minibus to Valbona (one service daily, journey time 45mins) – otherwise, a taxi from Bajram Curri to Valbona will cost around €25. Valbona is scattered along the valley for several kilometres, so let the bus/taxi driver know the name of the guesthouse you're staying at to make sure you get dropped off nearby.

Other routes

Slightly less conveniently for the Peaks of the Balkans Trail but handy if you plan to spend some time on the Montenegrin coast, Easyjet (www. easyjet.com) fly direct from the UK to Tivat, as do Norwegian (www. norwegian.com). From Tivat airport get a bus or taxi to Kotor, followed by a bus to Podgorica, and continue as above.

Flights to Pristina (Kosovo)

Wizz Air (www.wizzair.com) flies direct from London Luton to Pristina in Kosovo four times a week. Easyjet (www.easyjet.com) also flies to Pristina from several European cities, although not from the UK at the time of writing (2023). If you need to stay a night in Pristina, Hotel Prishtina Backpackers are located in the city centre and are reasonably priced (www.booking.com/hotel/xk/prishtina-backpackers.en-gb.html). From Pristina, take a bus to Pejë and another into the Rugova Valley (see below). This is actually the shortest route to get to the Peaks of the Balkans Trail.

Pristina airport

Pristina Airport (www.limakkosovo. aero/, called Adem Jashari) lies around 15km southwest of Pristina. There is no airport shuttle bus service, but a taxi into town will cost you around €15 (www.taxibeki.net).

Pristina to Pejë and the Rugova Valley

There are buses as frequently as every 20mins from Pristina to Pejë (journey time 2hrs), from where (in 2017) there were twice-daily buses to the Rugova Valley, where you join the Peaks of the Balkans Trail.

Pejë (Peć)

The main bus station is on Adem Jashari, about 10min walk northeast of the town centre. There are regular buses to Pristina. If you need to stop for the night in Pejë, Hotel Çardak (Mbretëresha Teutë 101; tel +386 (0)49 801 108, www.facebook.com/hotel-cardak) is a good, reasonably priced hotel in the town centre, between the main post office and the bus station. For tourist Information see www. pejatourism.org.

Pristina to Valbona

There are frequent buses from Pristina to Gjakova (in Kosovo, journey time 90mins), from where there are buses to Bajram Curri in Albania and from there to Valbona (see above).

Flights to Tirana (Albania)

For those starting/finishing the route in Albania, British Airways (www.britishairways.com) flies direct to Tirana, from where there are buses to Bajram Curri (5hrs) and from there to Valbona (45mins). Choose Balkans run a daily jeep to Valbona, departing from Tirana in the morning (tel +355 (0)69 88 01 181; choosebalkans.com). Alternatively, a taxi transfer from Tirana to Theth or Valbona will cost up to €150.

Tirana airport

Tirana airport (www.tirana-airport.com) lies 17km northwest of the city centre. There's a bus service into the city centre, otherwise a taxi will cost around €20.

Tirana to Valbona

There are several buses leaving Tirana for Baram Curri in the morning and early afternoon (journey time 5hrs), usually travelling via Prizren and Gjakova in Kosovo since the roads are better there, rather than all through Albania. Buses depart from Rruga e Durresit (the same street as the airport bus), just northwest of the Zogu i Zi roundabout in Tirana. From Bajran Curri there's a daily minibus to Valbona (journey time around 45mins), departing from Bajram

The Valbona Pass, looking towards the Valbona Valley (Stage 1)

Curri early afternoon (and returning from Valbona early in the morning). See 'Podgorica to Theth or Valbona', above, for more information.

Arriving by train
Podgorica is on the railway line between Belgrade, Serbia (from where there are rail links to Croatia and elsewhere in Europe) and Bar (from where there are ferries to Italy) – a rather spectacular journey in itself as it navigates a course through the mountains of Montenegro through a succession of tunnels and viaducts. The main railway station in Podgorica is located next to the bus station. For train timetables see www.zcg-prevoz.me.

For those considering travelling from elsewhere in Europe by train, Interrail passes (www.interrail.eu, see 'Global Pass') cover Kosovo (still listed as part of Serbia) as well as Montenegro, although not Albania.

Hitchhiking
Locals will usually pick hikers up on mountain roads, in particular in Albania and Kosovo.

ACCOMMODATION AND FOOD

Accommodation along the Peaks of the Balkans is provided by small village guesthouses, many of them outstanding, offering wonderful food and hospitality. Bedding is provided (sheets, blankets, pillows), so there's no need to carry a sleeping bag – although it's a good idea to carry a lightweight silk or cotton sleeping bag for use on a couple of the overnights where sleeping facilities are more basic, such as at Dobërdol (where sheets are not provided). Prices for staying in guesthouses are generally between €20 and €45 per person B&B (2023), but it's really worth getting half-board (€8–€10 per person extra) as the food is excellent – and in any case, if it's a village guesthouse it is likely to be the only place to eat anyway.

Meals at village guesthouses are usually prepared with fresh, local produce. Salads made from cucumber, tomato and onion; stuffed peppers; green beans simmered in milk; crumbly white cheese; grilled vegetables; simple but delicious stews; fresh village bread; homemade jams – these are just some of the things the author has been served during visits to Prokletije. However, that being said, the sheer numbers on the trail due in part to large group bookings by overseas tour operators, means that the quality of food has dropped in some guesthouses in recent years, sadly. As well as dinner, bed and breakfast, half-board in village guesthouses on the Peaks of the Balkans Trail usually includes a packed lunch, as well as Turkish coffee, tea (both of these generally in unlimited quantities, within reason) and homemade *rakija* – a potent local spirit. In guesthouses in Albania and Kosovo you should find plenty of vegetarian dishes (see Appendix D for how to

35

Tea at Kujtim Gocaj Guesthouse, Çeremi, Albania (Stage 2)

say 'I'm vegetarian' in Albanian and Montenegrin).

Mobile phone coverage doesn't extend to some of the villages on the Trail – meaning that in some cases it's simply not possible to call and book a bed at a guesthouse in advance. If you're trying to contact a guesthouse and there's no signal (for places where there's no mobile coverage, phone numbers have not been included in this guide), your best bet is to contact one of the local agencies listed in this guide (Zalaz or Zbulo – see 'Local tour operators'), and for a small fee they will get one of their guides to make the booking for you in person when they're next staying at the guesthouse with a group. Alternatively you can just turn up and hope for the best, but in July/August you might find places full – in which case the guesthouse may be able to help you find an alternative, but in some of the smaller settlements along the Trail there simply aren't very many places to stay.

Camping is possible on the Trail – some guesthouses have campsites (with the obvious advantage that you can have dinner at the guesthouse), and there are various points along the route suitable for wild camping (but note that camping within a national park or nature reserve is prohibited, which technically at least rules out almost the entire route in Montenegro). If camping and planning to cook your own meals, bear in mind that the only place along the Trail where you can really restock on supplies is Plav (in some cases you can also buy produce such as fresh milk and cheese from shepherds in mountain settlements).

Village guesthouses are listed for each stage in this guidebook, as are some places where it's possible to wild camp. There are further accommodation options listed on booking.com.

In Albania you'll pass small basic cafés/bars at several points along the trail, where you can stop for a Turkish coffee or a cup of tea made from herbs and flowers from the surrounding mountains.

PUBLIC HOLIDAYS

Official public holidays in Albania, Kosovo and Montenegro – meaning everything will be shut and a reduced (Sunday) timetable will be in place for buses etc – are as follows (where they only take place in one country, this is noted):

Movable official holidays (possibly depending on the predominant religion of the area you are

1–2 January	New Year
7 January	Orthodox Christmas Day
17 February	Independence Day (Kosovo)
8 March	International Women's Day
14 March	Summer Day (Albania)
22 March	Bektashi Festival of Nevruz (Albania)
19 April	Constitution Day (Kosovo)
1–2 May	Labour Day
9 May	Victory in Europe Day (Montenegro)
21–2 May	Independence Day (Montenegro: commemorating Montenegro's referendum for independence in 2006)
13–14 July	Statehood Day (Montenegro: commemorating the recognition of Montenegro as an independent state at the Congress of Berlin in 1878)
15 August	Assumption of the Virgin Mary
19 October	Beatification of Mother Teresa Day (Albania)
19 November	Liberation Day (Albania: commemorating liberation at the end of WW2)
28 November	Independence Day (Albania, Kosovo)
29–30 November	Republic Day (Montenegro)
25 December	Christmas Day

in) include Good Friday and Easter Monday and Eid; other major religious holidays such as Whit Monday (Pentecost, 50 days after Easter Sunday) and All Saints (1 November) may also be observed. Holidays are generally moved to the following Monday if they fall at weekends, and some may be celebrated over two days.

Note that museums often close on Mondays.

LANGUAGE

English is spoken at some level by most people offering accommodation and other services catering to hikers along the Peaks of the Balkans Trail – at least one family member will speak English even in rural guesthouses, and the level of English spoken by guides is very high. However, away from those places you can expect fewer people to speak English. Any attempt to learn, and speak, at least some basic words and phrases in Montenegrin (in

Women collecting wildflowers, between Balqin and Dobërdol (Stage 3)

Montenegro) or Albanian (in Albania and Kosovo) will be appreciated enormously by locals. For more details on language, pronunciation and a glossary of common words and phrases see Appendix D.

Montenegrin (*crnogorski*) is essentially the same as Serbian (*srpski*), but since independence from Serbia in 2006 it has officially been called Montenegrin in Montenegro. It is a South Slavonic language, closely related to Serbian, Croatian and Bosnian, and is written in both the Latin and Cyrillic alphabets – you'll find most menus and other things you need are usually written in the former. Serbian along with Croatian formed the base of the amalgamated (or 'standardised') language spoken in the former Yugoslavia, called Serbo-Croat.

Albanian (*shqip*) is an Indo-European language and is an isolate – that is, no other extant language shares the same branch of the Indo-European languages. There are two main dialects: *Tosk*, which is spoken in the southern half of the country, and which since WW2 has formed the basis of standard Albanian; and *Gheg* which is spoken in the northern half of the country, and is therefore the version most common in the areas visited by the Peaks of the Balkans Trail. Serbian is also spoken in other parts of Kosovo but the areas visited by the Trail are primarily Albanian speaking.

MONEY

The currency in Montenegro and in Kosovo is the Euro (€); in Albania it's the *Lek*.

You will find ATMs in larger towns and cities but obviously not in small mountain villages along the Peaks of the Balkans Trail, and while you can use credit cards at hotels etc in major cities and towns you should assume that you won't be able to use them to pay for food or accommodation along the route – which effectively means you'll need to carry enough cash to cover your entire trek. Carry plenty of small bills, and don't keep all your money in one place. The only places you can expect to find an ATM to 'top up' your wallet along the Trail are Plav and Gusinje (and with a short detour by bus or taxi, Pejë).

Costs

Albania, Kosovo and Montenegro are cheap countries to travel in by western European standards, with Albania and Kosovo being cheaper than Montenegro. How much you need to budget for per day while hiking the Peaks of the Balkans Trail obviously depends on whether you're staying in guesthouses or camping, and also whether you're hiking individually or have organised accommodation, guides and baggage transfers through a tour operator.

As a rule of thumb, staying in local village guesthouses will cost between €20 and €45 per person for B&B, an additional €8–€10 for half-board. Camping (at a campsite or guesthouse) is usually around €5. Drinks (including alcohol) and snacks are also inexpensive. In the capitals Podgorica, Pristina and Tirana you can expect prices to be higher than in villages and small towns along or near the Trail. Bus fares are very reasonable. Getting a cross-border permit yourself costs €10 or more in Montenegro (an additional €3 per person), but is free if you're starting from Albania or Kosovo. If you get it through a local tour operator, like Zbulo or Zalaz, it's €5 per person per border crossing (three crossings cover the standard route), plus €10 to cover the cost of the permit from Montenegro (€50 is the upper limit for a group of up to 20 and/or 6 permits, excluding the Montenegrin fee, so that's the most you'd end up paying; prices as at 2023). Hiring a local hiking guide costs around €80 per day; baggage transfers arranged through

Looking towards the Prosllopit Pass and Maja Kolata from Bajrak (Stage 9)

Zbulo or Zalaz cost around €50 per day (for a packhorse carrying four 4 bags up to 15kg), or around €200 per person as part of a 10–12 day guided walk.

So, for two people hiking without a guide, carrying their own packs and staying and eating in local guesthouses, with packed lunch and a stop somewhere for coffee, you can expect to pay between €30 and €55 per person per day, or thereabouts, while hiking the Trail. Wild camping obviously brings costs down considerably but you'd miss out on the delicious local cuisine and wonderfully warm hospitality – nor would you contribute to the local economy of these mountain villages which, within a remarkably short period of time, have made a concerted effort to make their spectacularly beautiful landscape accessible to foreign hikers.

Phone numbers

The international dialling codes for Albania, Kosovo and Montenegro are as follows:

- Albania +355
- Kosovo +383
- Montenegro +382

Local area codes and mobile numbers start with a zero, which should be omitted if calling from a UK or other overseas mobile or overseas landline – for example the local area code for Plav is 051, but from an overseas mobile dial +382 51 followed by the six-digit number.

Mobile phone signal

Mobile phone signal is limited to some of the larger villages and settlements along the Peaks of the Balkans Trail,

Horses grazing near Dobërdol (Stage 4)

Old border marker on the Borit Pass, on the border between Albania and Montenegro (Stage 2)

and in some places is absent entirely. You can also expect mobile signal to vanish much of the time when you're hiking between the beginning and end of a stage between two villages. For example, while you'll get a signal in Theth or Valbona, you'll only get a very faint signal (if you're lucky) at Babino polje, and you won't get any signal at Dobërdol or between the Prosllopit Pass and Çeremi.

Wi-fi

Guesthouses in some of the larger villages along the route such as Theth and Valbona often (but not always) have wi-fi for guests; in smaller settlements such as Çeremi and Dobërdol, there will be no internet (and possibly no phone signal).

Electricity

Montenegro, Albania and Kosovo all use the same, round two-pin plugs

(220V/50Hz) as found in most of the rest of mainland Europe.

CROSS-BORDER PERMITS

The Peaks of the Balkans route involves crossing backwards and forwards over several mountain passes between Albania, Montenegro and Kosovo. All hikers doing the Trail are required to obtain a special cross-border permit before they begin the route, from the relevant authorities in whichever of the three countries you plan to start from. You can apply for the permit yourself, however it is strongly suggested that you make your life easier by paying a local tour operator (currently Zbulo in Albania, see 'Local tour operators' below for contact details) to arrange the permit for you. Zbulo have a nice, clear, up-to-date summary of the procedure and pricing on their website (zbulo.org

41

and click on 'Border Crossings'): €5 per person per border crossing, plus the fee levied by Montenegro (€10 plus €3 for each additional person), with a maximum upper limit of €50 – as well as the relevant forms which you can fill in online. All that then remains is for them to send you a copy of the permit which you can print out at home, if starting the route from either Albania or Kosovo; or for you to walk into the Border Police office in Plav and pick up your permit, with no need to go to a local bank to pay the fee (see below).

The cost of the permit is €10 plus €3 for each additional person (2023) in Montenegro, but it's free in Albania and Kosovo. To make things just a little bit more time-consuming (at least when you start the route in Montenegro), you are not allowed to pay for the permit at the Border Police office in Plav, or online – payment can only be made at a local bank in Plav (the best one to use, where they're familiar with the process, is Atlas Banka AD, which if you're walking south from the bus station is near the top of the rise, shortly before the national park office), after which you must return to the Border Police office with your receipt, and pick up your permit. This means that, if starting in Montenegro and picking up your permit in Plav, you also need to factor banking hours into when you get your permit. (If you arrange your permits through an agency like Zbulo, they'll arrange for someone to make the payment for you, so all you need to do is go to the border police station.)

Bear in mind that on the application form you need to fill in the dates on which you plan to cross from one country to another (these are in theory not flexible, even though in practice changes in weather may delay you for a day). Also, although there is no checkpoint at any of the border crossings – the only indication you're likely to find that you've switched countries is an old concrete border marker – police do sometimes make an appearance (there's sometimes a Montenegrin police 4X4 parked near Čemerikino jezero on Stage 10, for example), so do make sure you have a printed copy of your permit with you.

Note that the Border Police (*Granična Policija*) office in Plav is not the same as the main police station (where they won't know what you're talking about – there has long been another registration system for visiting the nearby Grbaja Valley). The Border Police office is located on the northeast edge of town, on the road leading out towards Babino polje (most people won't be able to give you directions and will refer you back towards the main police station, which you really don't want): walk southeast from the bus station to the roundabout and the national park office (where they will be able to give you correct directions), straight ahead down the hill and left at the bottom, out past the cemetery.

The contact details for applying for the cross-border permit, for those who want to go it alone, are as follows:

- Albania: naim.byberi@asp.gov.al
- Kosovo: drejtoriapermigrim@kosovopolice.com
- Montenegro: ispgranicneberane@policija.me

Apply at least two weeks in advance through Zbulo; if you're applying yourself, allow longer (but, whether applying yourself or through an agency, not more than two months in advance – one month would be a sensible idea, as it would allow for you to apply through an agency if you don't get a response from the police within a couple of weeks).

You can download the application forms here: www.peaksofthebalkans.com/Cross-Border-Procedures.

However, many people find they simply don't get an answer when contacting the police themselves – and the contact details have been known to change. The page on cross-border procedures on the official Peaks of the Balkans website listed above has clearly not been updated for several years.

LOCAL TOUR OPERATORS

While you can arrange permits, self-guided or guided itineraries through an overseas agent, it's far better to do so through a local tour operator in Albania, Montenegro or Kosovo – their local knowledge and experience will obviously be infinitely greater, and you will help contribute directly to the local economy.

The following two operators, Zbulo and Zalaz (based in Albania

On the border ridge between Montenegro and Kosovo, near Qafa Bogices (Stage 4)

and Montenegro respectively), are both excellent. Very helpful and knowledgeable, they specialise in hiking and cultural tours in Albania/Montenegro/Kosovo (Zbulo covers the Peaks of the Balkans, Zalaz no longer does), and can arrange everything from cross-border permits to transfers, accommodation and guides. (Baggage transfers are arranged for guided groups, but are not always possible for individual hikers – it depends on the particular stage and access, and the availability of mobile coverage for that stage.) They were both directly involved in setting up the Trail, and their experience and knowledge of the route is unrivalled.

- Zbulo – zbulo.org; email welcome@zbulo.org; tel +355 (0)69 2121 612 or +355 (0)69 6731 932
- Zalaz – www.zalaz.me; email welcome@zalaz.me; tel +382 (0)69 314 222

Other local tour operators include:

- Journey to Valbona (www.journeytovalbona.com; tel +355 (0)67 3014 638): guesthouse in Valbona (Albania).
- Undiscovered Montenegro (www.undiscoveredmontenegro.com; tel +44 (0)20 3287 0015): based in Virpazar, by Lake Skadar (Montenegro), and run by a British couple who have lived there for years.
- Black Mountain (www.montenegroholiday.com): based in Herceg Novi (Montenegro).

- Outdoor Kosovo (https://outdoorkosova.com; tel +383 (0)49 168 566): based in Pejë.
- Balkan Natural Adventure (https://bnadventure.com): based in Pejë.

In any case, one thing to be wary of is that some non-local tour operators have begun using a truncated form of the actual Peaks of the Balkans route and sending in very large groups. This is unsustainable and is already causing problems with overloaded accommodation and a reduction in the quality of the food on offer.

WHERE TO START/FINISH

Since the Peaks of the Balkans Trail is a circular route, there are several options for where to start/end your trek. The most convenient (taking into account direct flights from the UK and local transport) are Theth in Albania, Plav in Montenegro or Rekë e Allagës in Kosovo (see the 'Getting there' section for details of flights and onward travel by local bus), the pros and cons of which are given below.

Starting from Theth or Valbona, Albania

- Direct low-budget flights from the UK to Podgorica (Montenegro) from where there are several possible routes to Theth or Valbona via Skhodër; direct flights from the UK to Tirana, bus from Tirana to Bajram Curri and from there to Valbona; direct low-budget fights from the UK to Pristina (Kosovo) from where there are frequent buses to Gjakova and from there to Bajram Curri, and from there to Valbona.

Pros
- Good trail markings on the initial stages (Theth–Valbona and Valbona–Çeremi).
- Of all the overnight stops along the Trail, Theth has one of the nicest guesthouses (Bujtina Polia) and you'll probably be more than happy to stay there a second time.
- Theth has some good excursions which you can add on at the end of your trip.
- If you apply for your cross-border permit through an agency, starting the Trail in Albania means you will simply be emailed a copy

which you can then print out at home (easier than the process in Montenegro).

Starting from Plav, Montenegro
- Direct low-budget flights to Podgorica from the UK, and several direct buses a day between Podgorica and Plav.

Pros
- Very good trail markings for the initial stages (Plav–Vusanje and Vusanje–Theth), both of which have spectacular views.
- Plav is the largest town on the Trail and has several supermarkets and shops where you can stock up on supplies.
- Plav has some good excursions which you can add to the end of

Autumn on Lake Plav (Stage 8)

your trip – in particular a visit to the Grbaja Valley.

Cons

• Plav–Vusanje begins with a long section walking on a 4WD road (but much of this can be skipped with a jeep transfer).

• Unlike starting the route in Albania or Kosovo, starting in Montenegro means picking up your cross-border permit from the Border Police office in Plav, and paying the fee into a bank in Plav, unless you've arranged the permit through an agency.

Starting from Rekë e Allagës, Kosovo

• Direct budget flights from the UK to Pristina, from where there are frequent buses to Pejë; from Pejë there are two buses daily along the Rugova Valley, from where you hike up to Rekë e Allagës (or you can take a taxi from Pejë or the Rugova Valley all the way to Rekë e Allagës).

Pros

• If you apply for your cross-border permit through an agency, starting the Trail in Kosovo means you will simply be emailed a copy which you can then print out at home (easier than the process in Montenegro).

Cons

• The trail is not so well marked on the stages in Kosovo.

While you can walk the route clockwise or anticlockwise, anticlockwise (as described here and on the Peaks of the Balkans Trail website) is preferable – for example the Pejë Pass on the Vusanje to Theth stage is far preferable as a descent rather than an ascent, while the steep climb on Bajrak on the stage between Plav and Vusanje is preferable as an ascent. Although the stages in this guidebook are numbered, this is more a matter convenience than anything else, in order to tie in with the order they are described on the GIZ map and on the Trail website – so there's nothing stopping you from starting with Stage 6 (for example) instead of Stage 1.

VARIATIONS, TRANSFERS AND HIGHLIGHTS

While the official route of the Peaks of the Balkans Trail has remained as it was when first mapped out, the route used on the ground, and that recommended by local guides and tour operators, has changed in a few places since then. Obviously you can still follow the full, 'official' 10-stage route as described on the GIZ map and Trail website, however you can also create alternative, shorter or – some would argue – more rewarding variations by skipping some of the sections along 4WD roads, and adding some of the spectacular areas nearby.

With this in mind, there are some suggested changes to the route in this guidebook. The 'official' stage between Valbona and Çeremi (Stage 2), most of which is along an asphalt road, is replaced with the much more rewarding hike between these villages over the Prosllopit Pass. A transfer between Drelaj and Restaurant Te Liqeni (Stage 6) along the asphalt road is advised, rather than hiking via Dugaivë (which is mostly along 4WD road and then through forest where in 2016 tractors and bulldozers were widening the few sections actually on a path, followed by a section hiking on an asphalt road) – although it's still worth stopping in Kuçishtë to see the church there. Also consider a jeep transfer between Plav and Feratovića katun, or at least part of the way (the last section of the 4WD road is very rough and steep). If you have a free day to stop in Plav, make a trip to the Grbaja Valley.

For reference, the 'official' route is broken up into 10 stages as follows:

- Stage 1: Theth (Albania) – Valbona (Albania)
- Stage 2: Valbona (Albania) – Çeremi (Albania)
- Stage 3: Çeremi (Albania) – Dobërdol (Albania)
- Stage 4: Dobërdol (Albania) – Milishevc (Kosovo)
- Stage 5: Milishevc (Kosovo) – Rekë e Allagës (Kosovo)
- Stage 6: Rekë e Allagës (Kosovo) – Restaurant Te Liqeni (Kosovo)
- Stage 7: Restaurant Te Liqeni (Kosovo) – Babino polje (Montenegro)
- Stage 8: Babino polje (Montenegro) – Plav (Montenegro)
- Stage 9: Plav (Montenegro) – Vusanje (Montenegro)
- Stage 10: Vusanje (Montenegro) – Theth (Albania)

However, this book recommends slight adjustment of Stages 2, 6 and 7 as follows:

- Stage 1: Theth – Valbona
- Stage 2: Valbona – Çeremi (via Prosllopit Pass)
- Stage 3: Çeremi – Dobërdol
- Stage 4: Dobërdol – Milishevc
- Stage 5: Milishevc – Rekë e Allagës
- Stage 6: Rekë e Allagës – Drelaj (this is short enough that it can be combined with Stage 5, if preferred, although you will need to get a transfer from Rugova Camp to Rekë e Allagës)
- Stage 7: (with a transfer from Drelaj to Restaurant Te Liqeni) Restaurant Te Liqeni – Babino polje
- Stage 8: Babino polje – Plav
- Stage 9: Plav – Vusanje
- Stage 10: Vusanje – Theth

This would make a 9- or 10-day trip, depending on whether you combine stages 5 and 6 in the same day. Consider adding on one or two extra days to visit the Grbaja Valley (from Plav) and Oko (from Theth).

For a shorter version of the Trail, it's possible to do a 7-day circuit via the Zavoj Pass, going down to Babino polje instead of on to Milishevc – although this largely misses out visiting Kosovo:

- Stage 1: Theth – Valbona
- Stage 2: Valbona – Çeremi via Prosllopit Pass

Looking towards the Ropojana Valley from the trail below Vrh Bora (Stage 9)

- Stage 3: Çeremi – Dobërdol
- Stage 4: Dobërdol – Babino polje via Zavoj Pass
- Stage 5: Babino polje – Plav
- Stage 6: Plav – Vusanje
- Stage 7: Vusanje – Theth

The most popular variation with tour operators and local guides is to start from Theth or Plav but go east from Dobërdol, climb Gjeravica, then (after a transfer) visit Pejë and Deçan with their UNESCO-listed cultural sites; before taking another transfer and continuing to hike some of the stages north of the Rugova Valley, then hiking from there to Babino polje; then missing out the Plav–Vusanje stage in favour of a day trip to the Grbaja Valley, before hiking from Vusanje back over the border to Theth, with a day trip from there to Oko – or some similar variation on the above.

However, some of this selection is based on what was in the past poor route markings between Plav and Vusanje – a section which was completely remarked in August 2016, and this is actually one of the most beautiful sections of the whole Peaks of the Balkans route.

Alternatively, for those who want to walk shorter days, on several (but not all) stages there is a convenient place to break the walk into two shorter stages, for example Theth–Rragrami and Rragrami–Valbona. If you're carrying a tent, you can obviously break the route up even further.

TRAIL MARKINGS

Trail markings in Montenegro and Kosovo follow the style used across the former Yugoslavia, and will be

Trail markings on the Pejë Pass, Albania (Stage 10)

familiar to anyone who has hiked in for example Croatia or Slovenia: a red and while bullseye marking or a red and white stripe (in both cases, red outside, white within). There may be 'arms' protruding from the bullseye indicating a change of direction, or this may be indicated by a bend in the stripe. In Albania and also in Kosovo a red and white rectangle is used (red without, white within). In either case, these simply tell you you're on a marked trail, not necessarily which one (or whether or not it's the Peaks of the Balkans Trail) – although the name of the destination may be added alongside.

There are also signposts in some areas (for example in Montenegro there is a good, uniform use of yellow signposts with routes and local trail numbers, as well as distances and timings). The Trail logo itself – three green peaks with a river flowing through them – appears only very occasionally on signposts or as part of trail markings.

Consistency and clarity of trail markings varies between different parts of the route – on some stages it is very clear, on others less so. In 2016, the stage with the least clear trail markings was the route between Milishevc and Rugova Camp. In general, trail markings are now excellent throughout the route in Montenegro, and for the first (westernmost) stages in Albania, while the easternmost stages in Albania and the stages in Kosovo are less clearly marked.

MAPS

A reasonably detailed map of the route at 1:60,000 is published by GIZ/ Huber and available locally as well

49

Map reading near the Zavoj Pass, on the border between Kosovo and Montenegro (Stage 4)

as through The Map Shop (www.the mapshop.co.uk) and Stanfords (http://www.stanfords.co.uk) in the UK. The map is generally good, at least for planning, although the scale is not quite sufficient for route finding and it has some major errors (for example a large section of the route on the stage between Dobërdol and Milishevc is completely inaccurate), and some of the alternative routes described in this guide (and used as the 'standard' route by local tour operators, for example the route from Valbona to Çeremi over the Prosllopit Pass) are not marked. Inaccuracies and discrepancies with the route as marked on the ground and described here are highlighted in the introduction to the relevant stage.

The map of Prokletije National Park (GTZ/Huber) covers a large part of the route at 1:50,000, but has similar inaccuracies to the Peaks of the Balkans Huber map. Vektor publish a 1:30,000 map of the Theth area and another at the same scale of Valbona. Frustrated with the inaccuracies on most maps, Caroline Bohne of Journey to Valbona is currently creating her own maps of local trails from open source base maps.

The Prokletije National Park Office in Plav is a good source of information and maps, for those starting their hike there. For more information on the Trail including route profiles and contacts, visit www.peaksofthebalkans.com.

EQUIPMENT

Most people considering tackling the Peaks of the Balkans Trail will be experienced hikers who will already have their own tried and trusted gear, however for those less familiar with hiking a route this long, the following checklist may prove useful:

- Rucksack – of sufficient capacity to fit all your gear
- Walking boots – either three season, or lighter-weight hiking shoes
- Walking socks
- Sandals or other footwear
- Rainproof, breathable shell
- Softshell jacket – preferably windproof
- Lightweight base layer – long-sleeved (more versatile than short-sleeved) hiking tops with thermal/wicking properties
- Hiking trousers – lightweight, fast-drying material, either with or without zips to convert them into shorts

- Other clothing – shirt, t-shirt, underwear
- Travel towel (lightweight and quick-drying material)
- Sheet sleeping bag/sleeping bag liner for use at Dobërdol
- Water filter – the Sawyer Mini (www.sawyer.com) is tiny and weighs a mere 56g
- Water flasks/pouches – collapsible plastic pouches weigh almost nothing and take up almost no space in your pack when empty
- Warm gloves and hat
- Sunhat, sunglasses, sunscreen
- Compass (even if you have one on a smart phone) and map(s)
- Torch/headlamp
- Small first aid kit (two knee-support bandages; fabric plaster strip for any blisters; non-stick wound dressings; small scissors, Swiss

On the trail to Dobërdol (Stage 3)

Ali Pasha Springs, an excursion from Vusanje (Stage 9)

Army knife or similar; alcohol wipes; small roll of surgical tape; tick remover; etc)
- Emergency reflective 'space' blanket, whistle
- Small two-pin adaptor (same as for most of continental Europe)

Optional:
- GPS
- Tent, sleeping bag and sleeping mat if you're camping
- Lightweight synthetic- or down-filled waistcoat (greater warmth to bulk ratio than a fleece) for cooler evenings

Trekking poles
Using trekking poles makes a huge difference to the amount of strain on your knees.

Pack trekking poles inside your rucksack when checking in luggage for a flight, at the centre or against the back frame of your pack, to avoid them getting bent. If they're too long to fit inside your pack, you can shorten them by removing the upper from the lower sections of the poles – keep the internal locking mechanism in place by wrapping a rubber band around it several times, and wrap the pointed ends to prevent them tearing your pack.

WATER

Despite this being a karst area, availability of water along the Peaks of the Balkans Trail is good – you can expect to pass a reliable spring with drinkable water at least once, or more, on each stage. Water is usually fine to drink from mountain springs without purifying, and is often channelled from the source to a tap or through a pipe. Don't assume that all those babbling mountain streams are as clean though: there is quite likely livestock in the area and in some cases (for example at Dobërdol) toilets are built directly over water channels so effluent is washed directly into streams. Carrying a small water filter such as the Sawyer Mini (see suggested kit checklist above), which takes up almost no space and weighs only 56g, is a good idea and gives you some

LOW IMPACT TREKKING

'When people destroy something replaceable made by mankind, they are called vandals; if they destroy something irreplaceable made by God, they are called developers.'

Joseph Wood Krutch

Beside Liqeni i Kuçishtës, Kosovo (Stage 7)

Large numbers of visitors inevitably place a degree of strain on the environment, from trail erosion to waste management. At the risk of sounding pedantic and stating the obvious:

1. **Carry all litter out of wilderness areas** – Although you will find litter bins at guesthouses in mountain settlements along the Peaks of the Balkans Trail, where possible try to carry your rubbish with you until you reach a town, out of the mountains. While someone will come and empty these at some point, in the meantime you have no control of this litter being blown away by the wind or dragged off by wildlife.

2. **Never light open fires** – Never light an open fire in the wild, due to the risk of forest fires.

3. **Keep to established trails** – Walking on either side of an established path simply widens it, increases erosion and damages surrounding plant life.

4. **Close gates behind you** – to prevent livestock wandering off.

5. **Use toilets at pensions, huts and restaurants** – It takes several months for toilet paper to fully decompose: use the toilets at pensions, huts and

restaurants, otherwise always bury toilet waste 15cm underground. Don't burn toilet paper.

6. **Avoid buying bottled water** – In the author's experience, the tap water is fine to drink in mountain villages and settlements along the Trail, as is the water from most springs; and bottles create waste, not all of which is going to be recycled. Carry a small filter such as a Sawyer Mini if you want to top up at springs along the route, and consider using it for the tap water in larger towns in Albania and Kosovo.

7. **Buy local produce where possible** – in doing so, you will support small businesses and the local economy.

more flexibility about where you collect water.

SAFETY IN THE MOUNTAINS AND WHAT TO DO IN AN EMERGENCY

Although the Peaks of the Balkans Trail is a relatively easy route with no technical difficulties – there are very few exposed sections, the trail is mostly well marked, and there are mountain villages offering food and lodging along the way – it is nevertheless very remote. A simple slip or sprain or a sudden change in weather has the potential to leave you stranded on high ground, possibly overnight, and anyone venturing into the mountains should be aware of the possible

The trail down from the Pejë Pass, Albania (Stage 10)

dangers, be prepared to administer basic first aid, and know how to react in an emergency. Unlike some of the more frequented mountain areas in Europe, if anything goes wrong in the remotest corner of Prokletije, you are likely to be on your own. As with any mountain walking destination, the following basic precautions should always be observed:

- Leave a description of your itinerary with someone at home
- Make a copy of the phone numbers of the relevant embassies in Albania, Kosovo and Montenegro (see Appendix A), and keep this separate from your passport, phone and other valuables
- Give details of your plans for the day to a guesthouse or other walkers
- Do not set off on high or exposed routes in bad or deteriorating weather
- Always carry adequate warm and waterproof clothing
- Always carry an adequate supply of food and water
- Always carry sufficient navigational aids – smart phone, GPS, compass, map(s) – and know how to use them
- Always carry a small first aid kit and an emergency bag or 'space blanket', a torch, and a small whistle for attracting attention
- Stick to established trails – while the route is free from landmines or unexploded ordnance, some surrounding areas have seen landmine deployment and airstrikes in recent conflicts, and while these have since been cleared, it is still prudent to stick to areas with established hiking trails
- In cold or extreme weather conditions, be alert to any of the symptoms of exposure or hypothermia: loss of coordination, slurred speech, numbness in hands and feet, shivering, shallow breathing or impaired vision. If hypothermia is suspected, get the victim out of the wind/rain, replace wet clothing with dry garments, keep the victim warm and give hot fluids and foods with high sugar and carbohydrate levels.
- Know the internationally recognised call for help: six visual or

---

Helicopter rescue
The following signals are used to communicate with a helicopter:

Help needed:
raise both arms
above head to
form a 'Y'

Help not needed:
raise one arm
above head, extend
other arm downward

audible signals (torch, whistle, etc) per minute, followed by a minute's pause, then repeated. The answer is three signals per minute followed by a minute's pause.

- Make sure your chosen insurance policy covers accidents in the mountains (many don't).

Emergency telephone numbers

In an emergency, call the European emergency number, 112. You can also contact emergency services in Albania, Kosovo and Montenegro using the following numbers:

Albania
- Police 192
- Ambulance 127

Montenegro
- Police 122

- Ambulance 124

Kosovo
- Police 192
- Ambulance 194

Mountain rescue

There is a mountain rescue service in Montenegro (Gorska Služba Spasavanja or GSS; www.gss-cg.me – English-language option available; tel 040 256 084). There is also a fledgling mountain rescue service in Valbona, Albania – Valobona MRS, which was set up through a local NGO, Shoqata e Akomodimit Valbone (contact Valbona Guesthouse on tel +355 (0)67 30 14 637 or +355 (0)67 30 14 638). In Kosovo there is a small mountain rescue team in Pejë (contact Balkan Natural Adventure tel +383 (0)49 661 105).

Local mountain guide and mountain rescue volunteer Ahmet Reković, in early morning frost at Katun Feratovića (Stage 9)

View towards Krš Bogićevica and Babino polje from the border ridge between Montenegro and Kosovo (Stage 4)

Never call for mountain rescue services in anything other than a genuine emergency. If you do need to call mountain rescue services, be prepared to supply the following information:

- Your name and the name of the person injured
- Nature of incident, the number of people involved, urgency
- Location of incident, including route name/approximate altitude
- Time
- Weather conditions, including wind and visibility

For more information see www.peaksofthebalkans.com/Mountain-Safety.

As well as trying to contact mountain rescue or emergency services, contact your embassy in Albania, Kosovo or Montenegro (see Appendix A).

At the time of writing (2023), emergency medical treatment for UK nationals was free in Montenegro (state medical care, not private medical care on providing a valid GHIC or EHIC card), but not in Albania and Kosovo.

Specific hazards

Snakebite

There are two species of venomous snake inhabiting the area covered by the Peaks of the Balkans Trail: the common viper or adder, and the nose-horned viper (see the 'Wildlife and plants' section). Snakes will usually bite only in self-defence (when you step on, or too near, them), however in the unlikely event that snakebite does occur, immobilise the limb or affected area, keep it below heart level, and get the victim to a doctor. Anti-venoms are available from hospitals and medical centres; sucking the wound and spitting has been shown to be completely ineffective. If possible, try to identify the snake in question, but take care to avoid getting bitten yourself.

Ticks

Ticks are present in the countries through which the Trail passes, and tick bites carry a risk of infection with European tick-borne encephalitis and Lyme disease (before that sets off too many alarm bells, the same can be said for several more frequently visited countries in Europe). A tick bite does not necessarily mean that you have become infected – not all ticks carry the bacteria leading to Lyme disease or European tick-borne encephalitis, and not all tick bites lead to infection. However, both are highly unpleasant, debilitating and in some cases, fatal diseases, and it's well worth knowing how to minimise your chances of contracting them.

The best form of protection against ticks is avoidance – wear long trousers when walking through the undergrowth or long grass, or through the forest, along with a hat, particularly in late spring or early summer (when ticks are at their most common). Check your skin and scalp when you finish your walk in the evening (a tick's body is brown and about the size of a pinhead).

In the event that you do find a tick attached to your skin, remove it as soon as possible – the risk of infection becomes higher if the tick remains undetected and is not removed within 24 hours. Ticks should be removed carefully using a special tick-removing tool such as O'Tom Tick Twister or the tick tool made by CarePlus (www.careplus.eu). Do not pull, squeeze or crush the tick's abdomen, or use irritants or cigarettes to encourage it to drop off you – doing so will cause it to regurgitate and therefore increase the risk of infection considerably. Instead, slip the head of the tick-tool under the tick's body, as close to your skin as possible, and twist gently. Once removed, clean the wound with alcohol or iodine, and make a note of the date you were bitten. A rash or fever a few days or more after the bite, or a red area spreading around the bite site, are signs that you may need further medical treatment. For more information about ticks and tick-borne diseases see the website of the British Mountaineering Council

---

LANDMINES

While the Peaks of the Balkans route is free from landmines or unexploded ordnance, some surrounding areas (for example some of the slopes of Gjeravica in Kosovo) have seen landmine deployment and/or airstrikes in recent conflicts, and while these have since been cleared, it is prudent to stick to areas with established hiking trails.

View back towards Bajrak from the trail to Vrh Bora (Stage 9)

(www.thebmc.co.uk/hill-skills-tick-alert) and www.tickalert.org.

General safety and security

In terms of general security, the mountains of Prokletije are a very safe place to travel. The people – Albanians, Montenegrins, Kosovars – living in the mountain villages of Prokletije are proud, hospitable and in the vast majority cases, scrupulously honest. Theft is rare. Nevertheless bear in mind that living conditions are hard and people here are generally very poor, so as much out of respect for this as anything else, and just as you would travelling anywhere else, avoid waving wads of cash and expensive camera gear around. In major cities away from the mountains such as Podgorica, Tirana and Pristina, consider the potential for pick-pocketing and petty theft as much of a reality as in most other major European cities, and exercise common sense accordingly. If travelling during the run-up to elections, it's worth checking Foreign Office advice pages, and where possible avoiding areas where any protests are planned.

Albania, Kosovo and Montenegro lie on areas of seismic activity. However, it's worth bearing in mind that while earthquakes and tremors do sometimes occur here, the risk (which is generally greater in large towns and cities) or likelihood is no greater than in other, better-known earthquake zones in Mediterranean Europe, such as Italy.

USING THIS GUIDE

Stage numbering

The stages are numbered purely out of convenience – since it's a circular route, you can start/finish at several different points (see 'Where to start/finish', above).

Difficulty

A short summary of the terrain and any particular difficulties encountered on a route is given in the box at the beginning of each stage, rather than a grade to indicate difficulty.

While a moderate level of fitness is assumed, the walking itself is not difficult – there are no sections that require any scrambling/climbing skills or equipment (although there are some parts that are quite steep), and the amount of ascent, the duration and the distances involved are moderate. The route follows established trails, the majority (but not all) of them clearly waymarked. However, bear in mind that you're hiking in an area that is very remote, and sudden changes in weather can make walking conditions, and route finding, considerably more difficult – see the section on mountain safety, above.

Timings and distances
The timing given in the box preceding each stage refers to an average walking speed, and does not include breaks or stopping time (as a general rule of thumb, add 10mins to every hour). Altitudes and distances are given in metres and kilometres throughout the guide.

Maps
The maps accompanying the route description in this guide have been prepared from open source mapping, not from the official Peaks of the Balkans Trail map (1:60,000) published by GIZ/Huber, which has some significant errors in some places and doesn't show all relevant trails. Therefore you'll find the maps in this guide differ in places from the GIZ/Huber one. The route maps in this guide are printed at a scale of 1:50,000.

Route description

Spelling and local place names
Place names are given in both English and the local name, according to which country the route is in at that point – for example Pejë Pass (Qafa e Pejë) in Albania. Where discrepancies occur in the spelling of place names between those on the ground and those on the official Peaks of the Balkans Trail map, they are highlighted in the information box at the start of each walk. For alternative spellings in Albanian using ë/a, the one used most commonly locally for that place/landmark has been adopted – so Valbona rather than Valbonë, but Pejë rather than Peja or Peć. English spelling has been used for place names that are already likely to be familiar (so, Montenegro not Crna Gora).

Abbreviations and landmarks
Within the route description, points of the compass are abbreviated to 'N', 'S' etc, and left and right to 'L', 'R'. Places or features along the way that are shown on the stage maps are represented in **bold** within the text, to aid navigation.

THE PEAKS OF THE BALKANS TRAIL

Looking south from the trail above Milishevc. The prominent peak is Marijash (Stage 5)

STAGE 1

Theth (Albania) – Valbona (Albania)

Start	Theth (728m, Albania)
Finish	Valbona (935m, Albania)
Distance	19.5km
Ascent/descent	1070m/850m
Time	8hrs
Terrain	Some 4WD walking between Theth and the start of the trail, and a 4km stretch on asphalt in the Valbona Valley; otherwise good, clear paths.
Highest point	1759m (Valbona Pass)
Maps	Valbona is also written Valbonë; Theth is also written Thethi
Access	Valbona can be reached by minibus or taxi from Bajram Curri, from where there are bus/ferry connections to Shkodër.
Food and lodging	Guesthouses and campsites in Valbona
Intermediate stops	Guesthouse at Rragrami

A beautiful stage, crossing the Valbona pass with spectacular views over the Valbona and Theth valleys. If possible, arrange a transfer back to the bridge at Okoli and start from there, to save hiking back along that section of 4WD from Theth. Valbona village is scattered over around 10km along the floor of the Valbona Valley, so the actual distance of this stage depends somewhat on where you choose to stay in Valbona.

THETH

For more information on Theth, see the end of Stage 10

Food and lodging

Bujtina Polia (tel +355 (0)67 526 7526 or +355 (0)66 666 9944; food served). Wonderful guesthouse with lovely, welcoming hosts and heavenly food. The owner, Pavlin Polia, was involved in marking out trails in the area and spearheading sustainable tourism in Theth when the Peaks of the Balkans Trail was being developed.

Shpella Guesthouse (tel +355 (0)69 377 4851; **www.booking.com/544379f048e939**; food served).

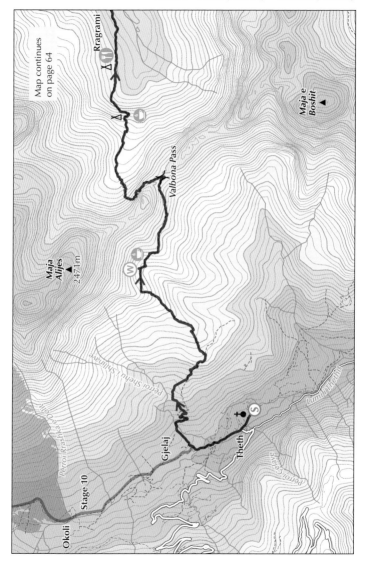

Map continues
on page 64

63

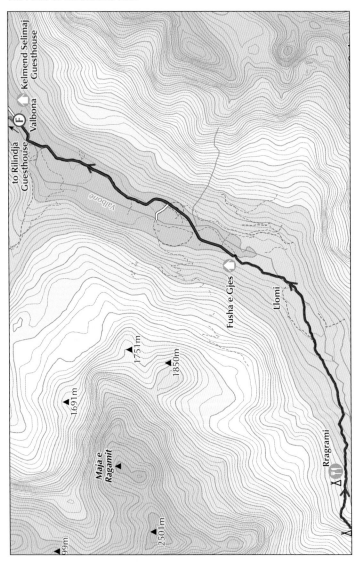

Guesthouse Pashko (**www.booking.com/hotel/al/guesthouse-pashko.en-gb.html**; food served). 200m SE of the church.

Villa Gjeçaj (**https://villagjecaj.com/our-rooms/**; food served). Near the road bridge.

Bujtina Leke Gerla (**www.booking.com/hotel/al/bujtina-leke-gerla.en-gb.html**; food served). 50M SW of Bujtina Polja.

Bujtina Kometa (**www.booking.com/hotel/al/bujtina-kometa.en-gb.html**; food served). Okol.

Kulla e Sadri Lukes (**www.booking.com/hotel/al/kullat-e-sadri-lukes.en-gb.html**; food served). Okol.

Info

For more information on Theth and its surroundings, see thethi-guide.com.

Transport

During summer there's a minibus from Theth to Shkodër. A taxi to Tirana costs around €120.

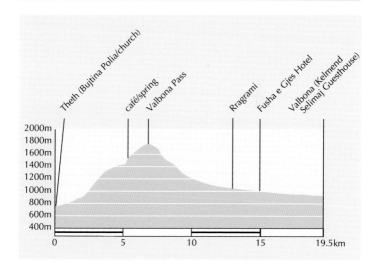

Looking south from the Valbona Pass

From the church and Bujtina Polia in Theth, go N along the 4WD road towards Okoli, (on the R bank of the river), then after going uphill opposite the bridge turn R where the 4WD road splits.

Follow this 4WD road uphill for an hour, then turn L off the 4WD just before a house (there's a sign pointing to a café/bar and a beer tub beside the trail) and follow a path steeply uphill, through forest. Where the path scatters, keep straight ahead.

An hour after leaving the 4WD road, enter a meadow, bearing R where the path splits. At the far (upper) side of the meadow, re-enter forest. The path contours the hillside before reaching a small stream in 30mins, and immediately after this a **café/bar** with a wooden terrace. Pass the café/bar on your L then go straight uphill and R through the forest again.

As the path emerges from the trees there are jaw-dropping views of Maja e Boshit (Maja Bošit, 2416m), the peak on your R. Continue up to the **Valbona Pass** (1759m), 3hrs 45mins after leaving the 4WD road. The pass gives unrestricted views north to Maja Jezerces, at 2694m the highest mountain in Prokletije, as well as east along the Valbona Valley, and west back towards Theth.

As you admire the view of the Valbona Valley, consider that there are plans – approved by the Albanian government, despite attempts by locals, the WWF and other organisations to oppose them – to construct a series of

hydroelectric power plants along a 30km stretch of the Valbona River, several of them within Valbona National Park itself. See 'Valbona River hydroelectric power plants' in this book's introduction.

Turn L from the pass and descend gradually NW, below crumbling cliffs (watch out for falling rocks) the base of which are carpeted with flowers. Follow the trail as it zigzags steeply downhill, passing a huge boulder then crossing a boulder-strewn dry stream bed, the trail marked by an occasional cairn.

Go along a clear trail through forest, then an hour from the Valbona Pass bear R to reach a small stream and a **café/bar** which also offers camping spots. Bear L above the café/bar, go steeply downhill (slippery) to reach another **café and campsite** by a stream, near **Rragrami**, 90mins from the Valbona Pass.

Follow a 4WD track downhill for a further 10mins to reach the broad, gravelly valley floor, by a signpost pointing back to Theth. Continue along the valley floor on a 4WD, initially faint then clearer, to arrive at the end of an asphalt road beside the large **Fusha e Gjes Hotel** in 45mins.

Go straight ahead along the asphalt road to reach the scattered houses of **Valbona** – the village is spread along the valley floor for around 10km. It takes 45mins from the start of the asphalt road to the Jezerca Guesthouse, which

Peaks above the Valbona Valley, from the Valbona Pass

is on your R soon after a large ruined building, shortly before the trail to the Prosllopit Pass (this central part of Valbona is called Valbona Qender); and a further 20mins to the Rilindja Guesthouse (an area of Valbona called Ququ i Valbonës).

VALBONA

Valbona village stretches around 10km along the valley floor and is on an asphalt road to Bajram Curri. Valbona National Park covers an area of 8000ha in the surrounding valley, walled in by peaks such as Maja Jezerces, Maja Rosit and Maja Kolata. For information on the current, potentially disastrous proposals to build 30 hydroelectric power plants on the Valbona River, eight of them in the national park itself, see 'National parks and nature reserves'.

Food and lodging

Bujtina Ahmetaj (tel +355 (0)67 322 9613; www.booking.com/hotel/al/bujtina-ahmetaj.en-gb.html; food served). E side of town towards Guesthouse Rilindija.

Bujtina Brahim Selimaj (www.booking.com/hotel/al/bujtina-brahim-selimaj.html; food served). N side of the river near the start of the Prosllopit Pass trail.

Guesthouse Mehmeti (www.booking.com/hotel/al/guesthouse-mehmeti.en-gb.html; food served). E side of town towards Guesthouse Rilindija.

Guesthouse Skender Selimaj (www.booking.com/hotel/al/guesthouse-skender-selimaj.en-gb.html; food served).

Rilindja Guesthouse (tel +355 (0)67 3014 637; www.journeytovalbona.com; food served). Run by an American/Albanian couple who have been at the forefront of establishing sustainable tourism in the area. E of town towards Çeremi.

Villas Jezerca (www.booking.com/hotel/al/villas-jezerca.en-gb.html; food served).

Info

The best source of tourist information in Valbona is the Rilindja Guesthouse.

Transport

A minibus leaves Valbona early in the morning for Bajram Curri.

STAGE 2

Valbona (Albania) – Çeremi (Albania) via the Prosllopit Pass

Start	Valbona (935m, Albania)
Finish	Çeremi (1220m, Albania)
Distance	14km; via Çeremi River: 11km
Ascent/descent	1200m/950m; via Çeremi River: 540m/380m
Time	7hrs 30mins; via Çeremi River: 4hrs 30mins
Terrain	Good paths, clearly marked for most of the route except the last part of the descent into Çeremi (although the route remains fairly obvious); short section of rocky karst formations to cross between the two passes. The alternative route features asphalt for 7km, then a marked path (steep in places), then 4WD road (alternatively, the path can be avoided by continuing further along the asphalt road to reach the 4WD road).
Highest point	2039m (Prosllopit Pass) or 1220m (Çeremi)
Maps	The route over the Prosllopit Pass is not marked on the GIZ map. The GIZ map marks the alternative route along the road, but not the fairly well-established shortcut from the Çeremi River bridge.
Access	No public transport to Çeremi.
Food and lodging	Handful of guesthouses in Çeremi
Intermediate stops	None. You could camp between the Prosllopit and Borit passes – there's a large level area reasonably near a spring.

There are two possible routes from Valbona to Çeremi: the 'low' (valley) route, as marked on the GIZ map (this follows the asphalt road for much of the way, so a transfer is preferable, followed by a short hike on a path and 4WD track – see 'Alternative route', below); or, infinitely more spectacular and as described here, the 'high' route via the Prosllopit Pass, crossing the border ridge back into Montenegro and skirting behind Maja Kolata, then crossing the Borit Pass and descending into Albania once more. There also used to be an old mule path from Valbona to Çeremi but this was destroyed in a storm several years ago.

The Prosllopit Pass (Qafa e Prosllopet) is a 2039m pass between Maja Rosit and Maja Kolata. Both of Maja Kolata's twin summits can be climbed from near the Prosllopit Pass, but this would add another 500m of (in places difficult and exposed) ascent/descent to an already long day, so you would need to start very early or split this into two stages, with a night camped up beyond the Prosllopit Pass.

The route over the Prosllopit Pass is clear and well marked (although it's not shown on the official GIZ map), and is the way most fit guided groups are taken. In case of poor weather, the valley route is a sensible alternative (see below).

Note that there is no mobile phone signal in Çeremi – you'll lose signal before the Prosllopit Pass.

The Prosllopit Pass route starts from the main road in **Valbona**, just 100m E of and opposite the driveway to Kelmend Selimaj Guesthouse & Jezerces Restaurant, and is marked by an information board and sign to Maja Kolata. Cross the bridge and go L onto the 4WD track, then R onto a marked path which leads steeply uphill, up a rocky gully and through scattered forest. As well as the more familiar red and

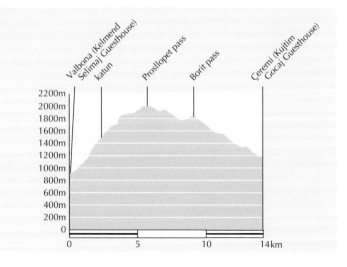

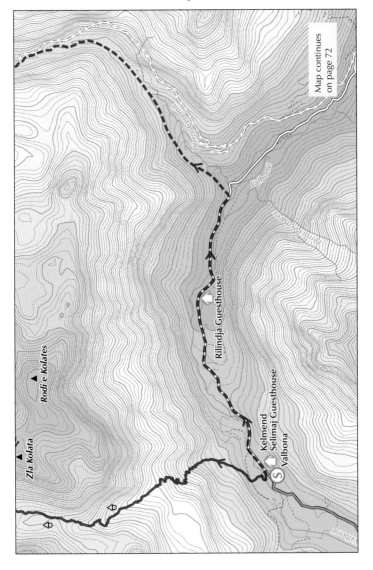

Map continues on page 72

Rilindja Guesthouse

Kelmend
Selimaj Guesthouse
Valbona

Rodi e Kolates

Zla Kolata

Valbonë

Perroi i Çeremit

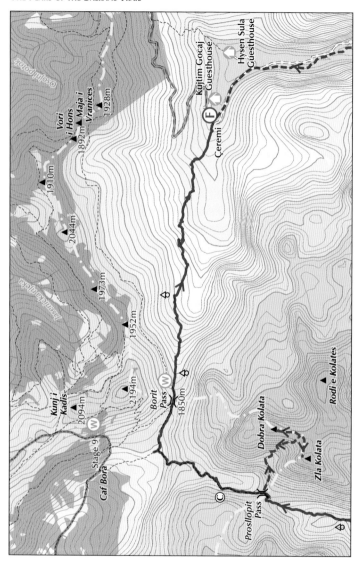

white trail markings there are some yellow and red markings here, and the trail passes a large wooden bench.

Some 2hrs from the main road the path enters a meadow and descends slightly to a level grassy area (possible camping, but no water) with an old shepherd's hut (*katun*) and a clear view of the peaks ahead on the border ridge, with Maja Kolata looming above you on your R.

> A *stan* or *katun* is a **summer settlement** in the mountains, to which locals move during the summer months to graze livestock in high pastures once the snow melts. You'll pass several of these on the Peaks of the Balkans Trail – some still occupied during summer months, some now permanently abandoned.

Continue straight across the grassy area and up through old forest, then over open slopes with profuse wildflowers and on the author's visit in early August, clouds of small blue butterflies. About 45mins from the shepherd's hut you reach a saddle with an abandoned stan. Continue upwards and bear R – the trail itself is quite faint but the markings are there.

Cross a shoulder and descend slightly and continue over a level grassy area (possible camping, but no water), passing a small very dirty pond on your R (this is described as polluted by locals, so don't take water from here even if you're purifying it). Continue uphill to reach the **Prosllopit Pass** (2039m), 4hrs from the main road.

Prosllopit Pass, on the border between Albania and Montenegro

Detour to climb Maja Kolata

The Prosllopit Pass is the main approach route for climbing Maja Kolata (2534m), the highest mountain in Montenegro, which towers above you on your R (E). While the route from the Prosllopit Pass can be undertaken by experienced trekkers, it's a more difficult route than the Peaks of the Balkans Trail, and Maja Kolata should not be underestimated – there are some exposed sections, the trail is not very clear, and the weather can change in Prokletije notoriously quickly. Maja Kolata has claimed several lives in recent years. In any case it would make a very long day as part of Stage 2, with an additional 500m of ascent, so it is better considered with a night camped below the Prosllopit Pass.

The route starts from the N side of the pass and goes ESE (unclear and very exposed in places) then SE, becoming steeper until reaching a col on the Montenegrin-Albanian border between the twin summits, Zla Kolata (Kolata e Keqe, 2534m) to the SW, and Dobra Kolata (Kolata e Mirë, 2528m) to the N. A third, higher summit, Maja e Koljats (Rodi e Kolates, 2556m), which is located entirely in Albania, can be reached by continuing further SE from the col.

Go straight ahead from the pass (you are now in Montenegro, although there's no border marker here), following a clear path down across the L slope of a large karst depression. After 20mins pass a **cave** (Ledena s Pecem) with snow inside right through the summer on your L, then cross a rocky karst area with a couple of steep, slightly exposed sections to clamber down.

Descend towards a large, level grassy area, which you reach 1hr from the Prosllopit Pass, by a junction which is close to the trail from Stage 9 between Plav and Vusanje (from this junction you can reach Vrh Bora in around 90mins). Camping is possible here, although there's no water and the area is used for grazing livestock – the nearest spring is 15mins along the trail towards Vrh Bora (see Stage 9).

Go straight ahead (NE) past the junction (no trail marking initially), up over some rocks then bear R and uphill to reach the **Borit Pass** (Qafa e Borit, 1850m), 25mins from the junction. The Borit Pass is on the border with Albania, and there's an old concrete border marker here.

From the pass, descend into Albania again following a clear trail down a gully, towards a stan. Keep on the L side of the gully and pass the stan on your R, crossing a stream which comes down from your L. A short distance past this there's a **spring** on your L. After the spring bear R and head downhill towards the stream to pick up the trail markings again, and turn L.

Where the path splits, take the R fork, then after this pass a large stan on your L and head downhill across a meadow, then into the forest again. Bear R again where the path forks, downhill with no markings initially and quite steep. Cross

Peak tower above the route from the Valbona valley up to the Prosllopit Pass, Albania

a stream, then follow a clear but unmarked path across meadows and downhill, with the first, upper house of Çeremi eventually coming into view on your L.

With a ravine on your R, follow a spur then bear L downhill to a 4WD track. Turn L onto this, to arrive in the upper part of the village of **Çeremi**, 2hrs from the Borit Pass, where you'll find the welcoming **Kujtim Gocaj Guesthouse** on your R.

ÇEREMI

Çeremi (the Ç is pronounced 'ch') is a small village on the bend of a small tributary of the Valbona River, close to the Montenegrin border.

Food and lodging

Kujtim Gocaj Guesthouse (tel +355 (0)69 411 2739, but no mobile signal in Çeremi; food served). Very friendly, welcoming guesthouse with delicious food, and close to where the trail down from the Prosllopit Pass reaches the village.

Hysen Sula Guesthouse (food served). Around 15mins SE along the 4WD road towards the Valbona-Bajram Curri road.

Vita Guesthouse (**www.booking.com/hotel/al/vita-guesthouse-bajram-curri.html**; food served). SE from Kujtim Gocaj, L bank of the river beyond the side stream.

Guesthouse Afrimi (tel +355 (0)68 2595 358; food served). L bank of the river, SE from Kujtim Gocaj.

The trail down to Çeremi, towards the end of the long descent from the Borit Pass

Alternative route from Valbona to Çeremi via the Çeremi River

This, the 'official' route of the Peaks of the Balkans Trail for this stage, is infinitely less interesting than the route over the Prosllopit Pass described above. However, in case of bad weather it provides a useful alternative. Try to arrange a taxi for the first 5km or so (depending on where you've spent the night in Valbona) along the asphalt road (about €10).

Either walk (allow 2hrs), or take a taxi, E along the main asphalt road from **Valbona**, as far as the bridge over the River Çeremi (Përroi i Çeremit) where a sign on your L marks the route to Çeremi. Turn L and follow the trail NE above the R bank of the River Çeremi (steep in places), then N along a 4WD road to arrive in **Çeremi**, 2hrs 30mins after leaving the asphalt road. **Kujtim Gocaj Guesthouse** is on the R just after a sharp bend to the R, shortly after the route from the Prosllopit Pass joins the 4WD road from the L.

STAGE 3
Çeremi (Albania) – Dobërdol (Albania)

Start	Çeremi (1220m, Albania)
Finish	Dobërdol (1820m, Albania)
Distance	15.5km
Ascent/descent	1030m/440m
Time	7hrs
Terrain	Some walking on 4WD roads, otherwise good paths with one fairly steep section.
Highest point	1920m
Access	No public transport to Dobërdol
Food and lodging	Guesthouse (food served) and mountain hut in Dobërdol
Intermediate stops	Balqin (tea, coffee and food)

This stage crosses into Montenegro then back into Albania, and ends at the remote settlement of Dobërdol, spectacularly situated below the triple-border point between Albania, Kosovo and Montenegro.

Note that there's no phone signal at Dobërdol, although you may pick up a signal briefly somewhere along the way from Çeremi.

Turn R from Kujtim Gocaj Guesthouse in **Çeremi** and follow the 4WD road uphill beside fields and orchards, with expansive views of Maja Kolata soon opening up to the E, and the route down from the Borit Pass visible. Pass a **spring** and cross several streams, before arriving at a small **café/bar** beside the 4WD road, a little over 1hr from Çeremi, with a spring opposite it.

Continue along the 4WD road, keeping straight ahead at a junction after 30mins, then after another 30mins arriving at an old concrete border marker, on the border with Montenegro. The letters 'RPSS' (Republika Popullore Socialiste e Shqipërisë) are inscribed on one side.

From the border marker, bear R following a path NE into the forest. Keep L where the path splits, then bear R up through a small, flower-filled meadow, to reach an open, grassy hillside. After a further 40mins, the increasingly steep path brings you to a saddle (**Qafa e Aljucit**) on the border with Albania, with a 4WD

Maja Kolata, from the 4WD road above Çeremi

track running across it. Go straight ahead over the saddle (and into Albania once more), following the path beside an area covered with blueberry bushes and passing a small wooden shelter on your L, and a slightly raised, rocky area on your R – a good place to stop for lunch, 3hrs from Çeremi, with views out over the valley.

> **Blueberries** grow in profusion along the Peaks of the Balkans Trail during July and August, at which time (as well as collecting them to eat yourself) you'll doubtless see many locals collecting them to sell on local markets.

Continue along the path, crossing several streams, and passing a **spring** on your L 30mins from the saddle. Just 5mins after the spring you reach the summer

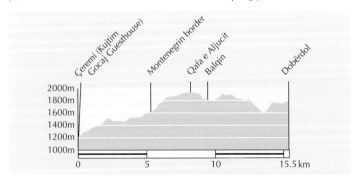

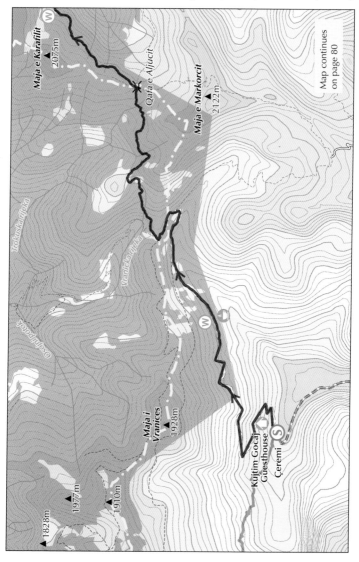

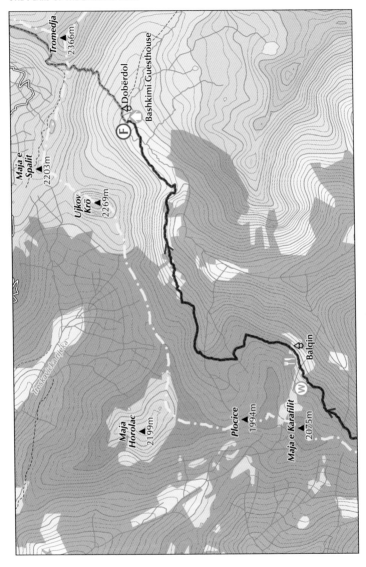

settlement at **Balqin**, 3hrs 40mins from Çeremi. The first house on your left offers coffee and other drinks, and can prepare food.

Follow the 4WD downhill then straight ahead (ENE) above the main cluster of cottages of Balqin. Ahead, there are views of the so-called 'Three Border Peak' (Tromedja, 2366m), and below this the summer settlement of Dobërdol. Cross a stream then turn R onto a 4WD track going downhill. When you reach the steam on your L, go down the second path on your L, cross the river and follow a narrow (loose in places) path above the L bank.

Turn R onto a 4WD track, pass two summer cottages then take a path on your L, which ascends steeply up the side of the valley to reach a shoulder. Go straight ahead along a 4WD track, descending towards Dobërdol. Turn L off the 4WD when you reach the river and follow the R bank for 5mins to reach a footbridge; cross this to arrive in the summer settlement of **Dobërdol**, 3hrs 20mins from Balqin.

DOBËRDOL

Dobërdol is a remote settlement used only during the summer months, in a beautiful location amid lush sloping pastures, below the point where the borders between Albania, Kosovo and Montenegro meet. While the 'official' Peaks of the Balkans route goes NE from Dobërdol, organised hiking tour groups tend to head SE, climbing Gjeravica and spending some time in Deçan and Pejë before taking a transfer and resuming the Trail in the Rugova Valley.

Use a water filter at Dobërdol, and definitely don't collect water from the streams as some have toilets built over them. With overly large groups in recent years overloading both accommodation and catering there have also been cases of norovirus (gastroenteritis). Beds and bedding at Dobërdol also tend to be fairly basic, so I'd recommend using a sheet sleeping bag.

Food and lodging

Bashkimi Guesthouse (tel +355 (0)67 456 1169, but no signal at Dobërdol; food served).

Dobërdol mountain hut. Basic hut, so a sheet sleeping bag is useful.

Bilbil Vatnika Guesthouse (**www.facebook.com/peaks.of.alps**; food served).

Bujtina Leonard (**www.facebook.com/BUJTINALEONARD/**; food served).

Sali Vatnikaj Guesthouse (tel +355 (0)68 3854 030)

Sokol Avdiaj Guesthouse (tel +355 (0)68 3762 668; **www.facebook.com/g.h.sokol.avdia?ref=hl**; food served).

Wildflowers near Qafa e Alujit, on the trail to Dobërdol

The mountain hut is on your R just after crossing the footbridge; to reach **Bashkimi Guesthouse** go past the mountain hut then L up the 4WD track for another 5mins – you can't really miss it, there's a huge sign at the front.

Excursion to Gjeravica

For those with time to spend an extra day at Dobërdol, the obvious excursion off the Peaks of the Balkans Trail itself is Gjeravica – at 2656m the highest peak in Kosovo and the second highest in Prokletije after Maja Jezerces, and a prominent landmark in this generally lower, eastern half of Prokletije. Gjeravica is more often climbed from Kožnjer in the north, but you can also climb it from Dobërdol. The route to the summit from Dobërdol is a straightforward hike, heading SE along the valley then up over the border ridge and into Kosovo.

A note of caution: Gjeravica is one of the few known areas near the Peaks of the Balkans Trail where landmines were deployed in the 1990s, mainly (according to the Kosovo Force) on the western slopes of the mountain. The landmines have since been cleared, and shepherds graze their flocks here, and plenty of hikers each year visit Gjeravica – but regardless of this, you should always stick to established hiking trails. Don't attempt this route in poor weather where route finding and orientation may become a problem, and consider going with a guide.

STAGE 4
Dobërdol (Albania) – Milishevc (Kosovo)

Start	Dobërdol (1820m, Albania)
Finish	Milishevc (1745m, Kosovo)
Distance	23km
Ascent/descent	1440m/1500m
Time	8hrs
Terrain	After a steep start, good paths for most of the way, but unclear trail markings in places.
Highest point	2258m (Roshkodol Pass)
Maps	The route for this stage shown on the GIZ map is completely inaccurate north of Qafa e Bogiqes – it is depicted too far east, whereas it should run up to and along the border with Montenegro, passing the Zavoj Pass (which is incorrectly marked as Ravno Brdo).
Access	No public transport to Dobërdol or Milishevc
Food and lodging	Guesthouses in Bjeshka e Zllonopojes and Milishevc
Intermediate stops	Aside from wild camping, the only possibilities for breaking this stage into two would involve either making a considerable detour (and descent) to Bjeshka e Belegut, or stopping at Roshkodol which is only slightly short of Milishevc anyway.

A fairly long stage with a fair amount of ascent/descent, climbing to the border ridge and crossing into Montenegro, then for a while following the border ridge before descending into Kosovo. Trail markings are unclear in places but the paths themselves are good, and the views are spectacular.

Note that a large part of the route differs completely from that shown on the GIZ map, which is out of date – this stage shares its route with that of Stage 7 for a short distance, turning the whole Peaks of the Balkans Trail into a figure of eight. Those wanting to create a shorter version of the Trail can turn west at the Zavoj pass and descend to Babino polje in Montenegro (see Stage 7 and Stage 8), instead of continuing to Milishevc.

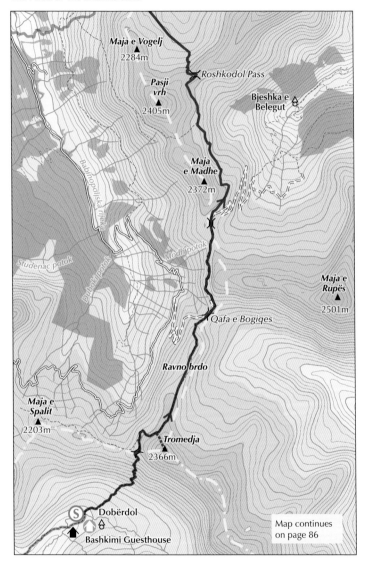

Maja e Vogelj
2284m

Pasji vrh
2405m

Roshkodol Pass

Bjeshka e Belegut

Maja e Madhe
2372m

Babinopoljska rijeka

Studenac potok

Dubski potok

Modri potok

Maja e Rupës
2501m

Qafa e Bogiqes

Ravno brdo

Maja e Spalit
2203m

Tromedja
2366m

Dobërdol

Bashkimi Guesthouse

Map continues on page 86

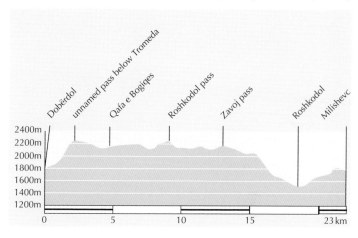

From **Dobërdol**, the route heads NE up to the obvious pass just L (W) of the prominent Three Border Peak (Tromedja). From Guesthouse Bashkimi, the most direct route is to follow the 4WD track E, then turn L and cross the river at the shallow ford, then begin climbing up the steep slope (there's no path initially), aiming for the pass and keeping slightly L of an eroded gully, to join a marked path coming up from the L. (If you've stayed at the mountain hut, you can also cross back over the footbridge, turn R and ascend gradually to pick up the marked path.)

Border ridge above Dobërdol, looking towards Hridski Krš and Babino polje in Montenegro

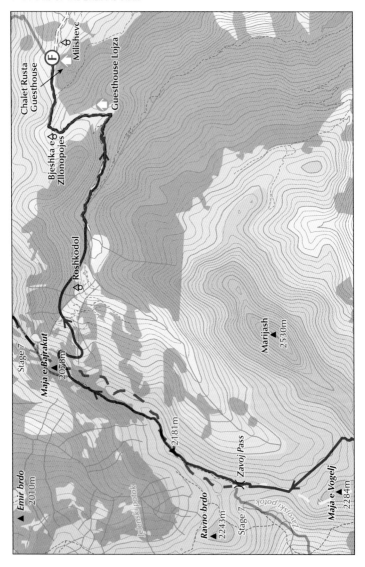

The trail down to Roshkodol and Milishevc from the border ridge

A little over 1hr from Guesthouse Bashkimi, you reach the narrow **pass** on the border with Montenegro, below **Tromedja**.

> **Views** from the pass are spectacular – northwest across Bogićevica to Hridski Krš (on the far side of which and invisible from here is Lake Hrid, which will be visited on Stage 8) and right of this, Babino polje; and south across Dobërdol.

Go R from the pass, then bear L (into Montenegro), behind Three Border Peak. The path is faint and rocky here, however within 25mins you reach a second pass, this time on the border between Montenegro and Kosovo.

Detour to climb the Three Border Peak
It's possible to climb the 2366m Tromedja ('Three Border Peak') from here, for enhanced views – allow 10mins to reach the top, following the steep, clear path SE from the pass, and 5mins to come back down the same way.

From the second pass, bear L and follow a lovely long grassy ridge (which marks the border between Montenegro and Kosovo), dotted with low blueberry bushes. There are plenty of spots suitable for camping, however there's no water and the ridge is very exposed to the wind. The prominent peak ahead, slightly R (E) of the ridge, is Maja e Rupës (2501m). Bear L and downhill to reach another pass, **Qafa e Bogiqes**, in 30mins, with a 4WD road, footpath sign and trail junction. (This 4WD road descends NW to Babino polje.)
  Follow the 4WD road straight ahead and uphill (signposted to Bjeshka e Belegut, and just L of the border ridge), and over another **pass** in 30mins, into Kosovo. From here the 4WD descends gradually into the valley, but soon after the pass and before losing much elevation, turn L onto a footpath marked only by a

cairn – this is not very clear and is easily missed (if you get to the first big hairpin on the 4WD road, you've gone too far).

The path itself is clear and trail markings soon resume. Descend slightly through a rocky area on the E slope of Maja e Madhe (not the W slope as described on the Peaks of the Balkans Trail website), before ascending again to reach the **Roshkodol Pass** (Qafa e Roshkodol, 2258m).

Descend from the pass, keeping L and above 2000m, heading almost due N. (There's a more direct, low level route down to Roshkodol from beyond the pass, which become clearer further down – useful in bad weather.) Go over a shoulder and keep straight ahead, ascending to the border ridge, which you reach a little over 2hrs from Qafa e Bogiqes. Plav is just visible to the west from here, and there are enhanced views from the slight rock outcrop next to the path.

Turn R (N) along the border ridge for another 20mins to reach a trail junction and signpost at the **Zavoj Pass** (Sedlo Zavoj, 2167m; marked on the GIZ map as Ravno Brdo), 5hrs from Dobërdol.

The path descending W into Montenegro from the Zavoj Pass leads to Babino polje in under 2hrs (see Stage 7). For now, continue straight ahead along the R (E) side and then along the top of the border ridge, to reach a trail junction in 1hr. Turn R here and follow the trail down fairly steeply for 1hr to **Roshkodol**. It's a further 1hr, following the 4WD road E then bearing L and ascending along the 4WD track to reach the small settlement of **Bjeshka e Zllonopojes** (Guesthouse Lojza is on the R (E) side of the 4WD track), then bearing R (E) and entering the W end of the pasture and summer settlement of **Milishevc**. Chalet Rusta Guesthouse is one of the first houses you come to on the R (S) side of the 4WD track, after the trees spread back from the road.

BJESHKA E ZLLONOPOJES AND MILISHEVC

Bjeshka e Zllonopojes and Milishevc are small, remote summer settlements east of and above Roshkodol. A rough 4WD track connects Milishevc with the main road through the Rugova Valley. Limited mobile signal.

Food and lodging

Guesthouse Lojza, Bjeshka e Zllonopojes (tel +386 (0)49 850 857, **www.face book.com/GuesthouseLOJZA**; food served)

Chalet Rusta Guesthouse, Milishevc (tel +377 (0)44 312 902, **www. facebook.com/ChaletRrustaMilishevc**; Adriatik_72@hotmail. com; food served).

Kula Guesthouse (**https://kullaguesthouse.com/**; food served).

STAGE 5
Milishevc (Kosovo) – Rekë e Allagës (Kosovo)

Start	Milishevc (1745m, Kosovo)
Finish	Rekë e Allagës (1300m, Kosovo)
Distance	16km
Ascent/descent	860m/1270m
Time	6hrs
Terrain	Difficult route finding at several points where trail markings are absent; 6km of road-walking between Rugova Camp and Rekë e Allagës, at first on asphalt then along a 4WD road.
Highest point	2136m
Maps	The GIZ map doesn't show enough detail for route finding. The position of Rugova Camp on the map is incorrect.
Access	No public transport to Milishevc; Milishevc is however accessible by 4WD road from near Pejë, which is fine for a 4X4 (so, a jeep transfer from Pejë would be possible, for around €50–€80).
Food and lodging	Guesthouse in Rekë e Allagës
Intermediate stops	Rugova Camp Hotel (food served)

This stage climbs to a high pass and visits a beautifully situated lake, Pusi i Magareve, before descending steeply into the Rugova Valley, a dramatic gorge slicing east to west between Pejë and the Čakor Pass on the border with Montenegro. The Rugova Valley was declared a national park in 2013, covering an area of 20,330ha. However there is opposition to the park from some locals, who fear it will affect their right to build houses there, to collect firewood and graze livestock in the area.

Several sections of this stage were still very poorly marked in 2016.

If you want to avoid the 6km of road walking between Rugova Camp and Rekë e Allagës, a jeep transfer will set you back around €15. If you decide to get a transfer, you should easily have enough time to continue hiking all the way to Drelaj, thus completing all of Stage 5 as well as the first half of Stage 6 in the same day – but it would be a shame to miss out on staying at Ariu Guesthouse.

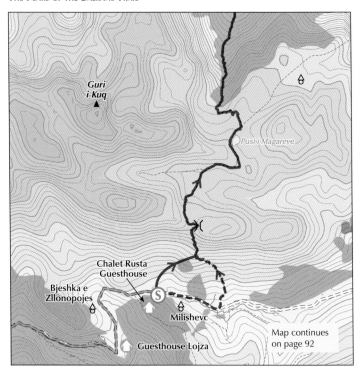

Follow the 4WD road uphill to reach the level meadow at the W end of **Milishevc**, if you've spent the night at Bjeshka e Zllonopojes; or if you've stayed in Milishevc, follow the 4WD road to the W end of the meadow, where there's a signpost pointing back towards Roshkodol.

Head NNE uphill on a marked path towards the ridge, where there appear to be two passes: one straight ahead up the slope, the other further to the right (E). The one to the R (E) is the one you want. The markings and path soon disappear, unfortunately, so just pick a way up around juniper patches and along livestock trails towards the pass, just below which you hit a clearly marked trail coming up from the far (E) end of Milishevc. Ascend on this trail to reach the unnamed **pass**, around 45mins from the 4WD road.

An apparently clear trail heads straight ahead (N) beyond the pass – but don't follow this, as it ends up boxed in by a wall of dense mountain pine above a steep-sided dell. Instead, look for a well-disguised path on your L almost immediately after the pass. Once you've found the start, the trail is clear and well marked, heading W along the base of the ridge until after 15mins you meet a trail coming down from your left.

Turn R and follow a faint, level trail across pasture, then bear L and slightly uphill on a clear path which takes you just to the L of a low, bushy knoll, before descending NW to **Pusi i Magareve**, a lake at 2113m with plenty of level areas to camp but no spring, 90 minutes from Milishevc.

Go L around the shore of the lake then straight up over a saddle, after which the route becomes unclear once more. Don't follow the clear, grassy 4WD track down to the R – instead, look straight ahead (roughly N) downhill towards the opening of the valley, below the cliffs on the E side of Gur i Kuq. Once you've located the lone marker pole there, head down to this then down further to your L from where you can pick up trail markings and a clear path once more.

The path down the valley is steep and slippery in places, but is quite clearly marked, and eventually becomes a rough 4WD track. Unfortunately trail markings disappear once more further down the valley. Follow the 4WD road past a house on your R, soon after which you pass a path on the R across a grassy area leading down a forested spur – do not take this trail; even though it is clearly marked initially it's very easy to miss the correct path, after which it eventually fizzles out above a very steep bluff. (If you're tempted to try the trail down the spur – a more direct route than continuing along the 4WD road, if you plan to stop at Rugova Camp – make sure you don't miss the point where the correct path

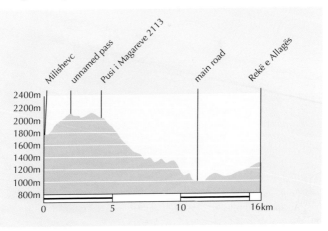

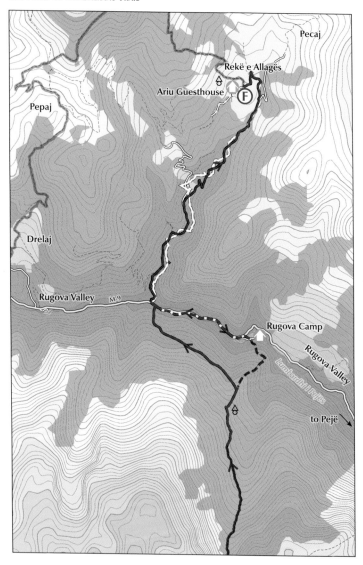

branches off to the left.) Instead follow the 4WD road all the way down to the reach the main asphalt road along the Rugova Valley, 1km W of Rugova Camp and around 3hrs 30mins from Milishevc.

Turn R along the asphalt road to reach a bridge on your L leading to a 4WD road. If you want to stop at **Rugova Camp**, continue past the bridge for another 1km; otherwise, turn L over the bridge and follow the 4WD road uphill towards Rekë e Allagës, passing a road on your L and taking the R fork where the 4WD road splits about halfway up (both roads lead to Rekë e Allagës, but the one on the R seems to be the one used by vehicles going up). In any case allow a little under 2hrs to hike the 6km from the asphalt road to Ariu Guesthouse (also known as Mustafa Hakaj Guesthouse) in the tiny settlement of **Rekë e Allagës**.

REKË E ALLAGËS

Rekë e Allagës is a small settlement above the Rugova Valley.

Food and lodging

Ariu Guesthouse (often called Mustafa Hakaj Guesthouse; tel +386 (0)49 867 098; food served). Stage 6 begins immediately behind the guesthouse.

Hostel Panorama (**www.booking.com/hotel/xk/peaks-of-the-balkans-trail-192-km.en-gb.html**; food served). N of Ariu Guesthouse.

Pushimorja Hajla (**https://hajla.al/**;). NE of of Hostel Panorama.

View from the trail above Milishevc

STAGE 6

Rekë e Allagës (Kosovo) – Drelaj or
Restaurant Te Liqeni (Kosovo)

Start	Rekë e Allagës (1300m, Kosovo)
Finish	Drelaj (1125m, Kosovo) or Restaurant Te Liqeni (1450m, Kosovo)
Distance	10km (Drelaj) or 23km (Restaurant Te Liqeni)
Ascent/descent	530m/710m (Drelaj) or 1260m/1140m (Restaurant Te Liqeni)
Time	3hrs 45mins (Drelaj) or 7hrs 30mins (Restaurant Te Liqeni)
Terrain	Paths initially then almost the whole stage is on 4WD roads, which still make for good walking above open slopes as far as Drelaj, but after that through forest and less interesting, much of it on 4WD roads and asphalt, with road building near Kuçishtë making route finding difficult. The last 4km is along an asphalt road.
Highest point	1820m (Qafa e Hajles)
Maps	A new asphalt road between Drelaj and Shkrel was being completed in 2016, and is therefore not marked on the GIZ map.
Access	There's a twice-daily bus from Pejë along the Rugova Valley; from the main road it's a 5km walk up a 4WD to Rekë e Allagës. A taxi or jeep transfer from Rugova Camp to Rekë e Allagës will cost around €15.
Food and lodging	Guesthouse in Drelaj (food served), hotel and restaurant in Liqenat i Kuçishtë
Intermediate stops	Guesthouses in Drelaj (food served); Hajla Mountain Cabin (off-route)

This stage climbs from Rekë e Allagës to a pass below Hajla peak, then follows a 4WD road across the hillsides above the Rugova Valley, before descending to Drelaj and the lovely Shquiponja Guesthouse. However, in summer 2016 a new asphalt road was being completed between Shkrel and Drelaj, and new forestry roads were being cleared along the section of trail between Dugaivë and Kuçishtë, making the only part of the route between Drelaj and Kuçishtë actually on paths rather than on 4WD roads quite unclear, and some of the paths were being enlarged into forest roads.

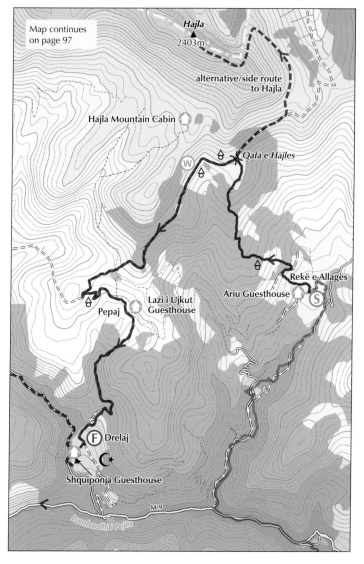

Map continues on page 97

Hajla
2403m

alternative/side route to Hajla

Hajla Mountain Cabin

W Qafa e Hajles

Reke e Allagës
Ariu Guesthouse S

Lazi i Ujkut Guesthouse

Pepaj

F Drelaj

Shquiponja Guesthouse

M-9

lumbardhi i Pejes

For this reason it is suggested that you skip the section between Drelaj and Kuçishtë, instead stopping at Drelaj (where there's a particularly nice guesthouse) for the night and then taking a transfer (about €15) from Drelaj to Restaurant Te Liqeni at the end of the asphalt road on Stage 7, and starting hiking again from there.

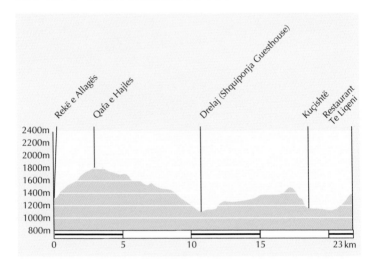

From behind Ariu Guesthouse in **Rekë e Allagës**, follow the clearly marked path that leads uphill through a field (the signpost at the beginning of the path marks Qafa e Hajles as 1hr 30mins away, but 2hrs is a more reasonable timing). Don't take the paths leading through gates on your L; instead keep going uphill (less clear) to reach a 4WD road and turn R along this.

Around 5mins along the 4WD road look for the start of a path on your L, and follow this uphill through pine forest and then open pasture with a fence on your R, and straight ahead over a farm track to reach a small wooden cottage. Keep going straight ahead uphill on a clearly marked path, bearing L then R, then keeping straight ahead with Ahmica (2272m, the peak E of Hajla) ahead. Once the path emerges into pasture go straight ahead over a slight rise, and then up to reach a 4WD road beside a small shelter and national park information board, at **Qafa e Hajles** (1820m), 2hrs from Rekë e Allagës.

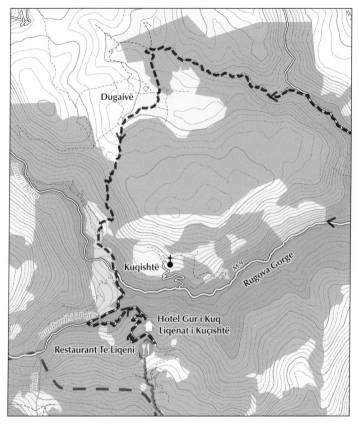

The recently designated Rugova Valley National Park faces hostility from some locals, who fear it will affect their ability to graze livestock and build houses in the area, and it's not unusual to find the words **'No Park'** scrawled across national park information boards.

(Note that Qafa e Hajles is also used to describe the slightly higher point further E along the 4WD road – a point which could more accurately be called a 'pass' than this one – and to confuse things further, a pass on the ridge N of here between Hajla and Ahmica. The GIZ map marks none of them. In this guide it is used to refer to the current location on the Peaks of the Balkans Trail, by the small shelter.)

Detour to climb Hajla

A path opposite the shelter leads straight ahead uphill to Maja e Hajles (Hajla, 2403m), a peak on the border with Montenegro overlooking the town of Rožaje (from where it's more often approached). If you want to climb Hajla from Qafa e Hajles (it's not on the Trail but is a fairly easy walk up), it's tempting to go almost due N to gain the ridge – but the most commonly used route is to follow the 4WD road R (E) for around 1km then turn L off this, bearing N then NW to meet the trail ascending the N side of the mountain from Gornji Bukelj and Rožaje; then S to gain the rocky ridge, which you then follow R (NW) to the summit of **Hajla**. Allow 2hrs to reach the summit from the Trail, and 90mins to return by the same route. The route is mostly unmarked. (Straying further onto the N side of the mountain would take you over the border into Montenegro, at a point which isn't included on your Trail permit, so is best avoided.)

If you're making a detour to climb Hajla, you might want to consider staying at the **Hajla Mountain Cabin**, which is on the hillside NW of Qafa e Hajles at the end of a 4WD track (but contact ERA, the local NGO which built the cabin, in advance to make sure it's open: www.facebook.com/eragroup).

From Qafa e Hajles, turn L along the 4WD road, passing a **spring** on your R after 15mins (and a sign marking that part of the 4WD road as 1776m), then follow the

Border ridge east of Hajla, from the trail to Qafa e Hajla

Shelter with picnic table at Pepaj (on the 4WD road leading to Koshutan, not the one leading to Drelaj!)

4WD road downhill to reach a crossroads in **Pepaj**, 45mins from Qafa e Hajles. Rather unhelpfully, among all the signposts at the crossroads, Drelaj isn't actually mentioned.

Don't go straight ahead, despite the way being very well marked with red and white trail blazes (but no further signposts), as this would lead you W to the new asphalt road between Shkrel and Drelaj. Instead, go L towards the Lazi i Ujkut Guesthouse (contact www.rugovaexperience.org) which you pass in around 20mins, continuing downhill to reach **Drelaj** in 1hr.

DRELAJ

Drelaj is a small village on the north side of the Rugova Valley, on the road to Koshutan which was enlarged and asphalted in 2016. The small mosque dates from the early 20th century. Shquiponja Guesthouse is down a road on your R, before reaching the mosque.

Food and lodging

Shquiponja Guesthouse (tel +386 (0)49 586 740; food served). Lovely welcoming guesthouse with excellent food. Minimal English spoken (and some French). The owner, Ilir Shala, will drive guests to Restaurant Te Liqeni for a small fee.

Peace House Rugova (**www.facebook.com/PeaceHouseRugove/**; food served).

Guesthouse Bujtina Kaçaku (www.facebook.com/profile.php?id=100075840322408; tel +383 48 142 758; food served).

Extension to Restaurant Te Liqeni

For those who still want to walk the 'official' section of this stage between Drelaj and Restaurant Te Liqeni: follow the road NW from Shquiponja Guesthouse to the village of Dugaivë, then go SW through a meadow, passing a short section affected by recent road construction in this area, and S through forest to the village of **Kuçishtë** (the route from Dugaivë to Kuçishtë was not at all clear at the time of writing), to reach the main road at a bridge. (Alternatively there's also forest path for some of the way – although it's only faintly marked. When leaving Drelaj, follow the road S for a short way instead of NW, then take a path on your R which meets the main trail at Dugaïve.) Follow the main road roughly S for around 1km then bear L uphill to **Hotel Gur-i Kuq**.

HOTEL GUR I KUQ AND RESTAURANT TE LIQENI

From the bus stop on the main road along the Rugova Valley, follow a secondary road, also asphalted, S and uphill to reach Hotel Gur i Kuq and beyond this, Restaurant Te Liqeni at the end of the asphalt.

Food and lodging

Prices for both these hotels are higher than most traditional guesthouses along the Peaks of the Balkans Trail.

Hotel Gur i Kuq (tel +386 (0)49 150 551; food served). Hotel with wooden cabins.

Hotel and Restaurant Te Liqeni. At the end of the asphalt road.

STAGE 7

Restaurant Te Liqeni (Kosovo) – Babino polje (Montenegro)

Start	Restaurant Te Liqeni (1450m, Kosovo)
Finish	Babino polje (1490m, Montenegro)
Distance	16km
Ascent/descent	1150m/1110m
Time	7hrs 30mins
Terrain	Although the route beyond the two lakes is often described as unclear, it's actually quite straightforward; only at one point on the ridge after the Jelenak Pass (Qafa e Jelenkut), where the trail markings imply that a path to the left is the only marked trail (it isn't) rather than the route straight ahead (which is the one you want), do things become unclear.
Highest point	2272m (Qafa e Jelenkut)
Maps	Liqeni Madhe is marked as Liqeni i Drelaive on the GIZ map, and the route between the border ridge and Roshkodol is also marked incorrectly. The Zavoj Pass is incorrectly marked as Ravno brdo.
Access	A local bus runs along the Rugova Valley from Pejë twice daily, and will pick up and drop off passengers at the bottom of the asphalt road leading up to Restaurant Te Liqeni.
Food and lodging	Guesthouse and mountain hut in Babino polje
Intermediate stops	None. If you need to camp, the nicest spot is a small unnamed lake on the border ridge between the Jelenak Pass and Maja Bajrakat, but there's no spring there (there's a spring at the saddle below the Jelenak Pass, Lugu i Shkodrës). For a more sheltered spot, there's a level area in the forest just above the path alongside Liqeni i Kuçishtës (but again, no spring).

A long but spectacularly beautiful stage, passing two attractive lakes before crossing the Jelenak Pass (Qafa e Jelenkut) – which, unless you're doing some peak-bagging along the route, marks the highest point on the Peaks of the Balkans Trail. The route then follows the border ridge, overlapping for a short distance with the route from Stage 4, before descending to Babino polje in Montenegro.

If you've spent the night at Drelaj and decided to skip the second half of Stage 6, a transfer from Drelaj to the end of the asphalt road at Restaurant Te Liqeni at the start of Stage 7 will cost around €15 (ask Ilir Shala, owner of Shquiponja Guesthouse).

From Restaurant Te Liqeni bear R and where the asphalt stops continue uphill along a 4WD road, ignoring a 4WD road branching off on your L. Turn R onto a path marked Liqeni Madhe, passing a **spring** on your L and on your R a fairly level area where it would be possible to camp.

Bear L up a path which becomes a 4WD, then turn R onto a marked path, passing a **spring** on your R and ascending. Go across a jumbled boulder field. Continue ascending with a prominent peak ahead and a ridge on your R, to reach a grassy saddle 1hr from Restaurant Te Liqeni, with the first lake, **Liqeni i Kuçishtës**, below you.

Walk down to the lake and turn L along the shore, signposted 'Liqeni i Vogel' (the route does not go up the steep slopes towards a pass on the opposite side of the lake – although having said that, the author did meet a group who had taken this route, following the ridge SE, with spectacular views, to rejoin the official route at the Jelenak Pass). Bear R at the end of the lake and follow the marked trail which descends, steeply in places with a short, slightly exposed section, to reach open pasture with a small shepherd's hut.

You're likely to see a large breed of mountain shepherd dog – the **Šarplaninac** (named after the Šar mountains on the border between Albania and

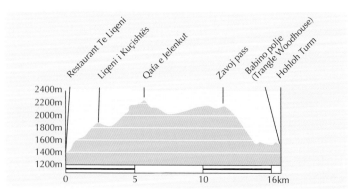

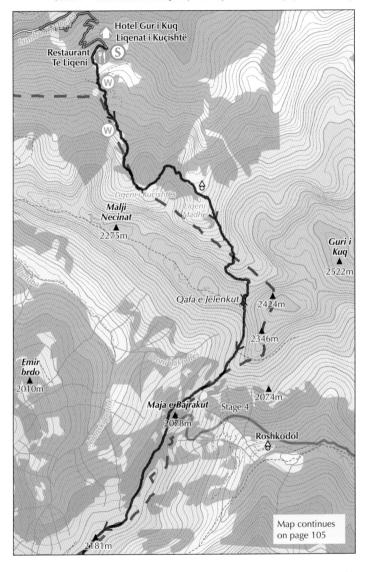

Map continues
on page 105

103

Macedonia) – on the Peaks of the Balkans Trail, guarding flocks. As with any sheepdog, avoid walking between the dog and the flock it's guarding.

Turn R and go uphill with a stream on your L and a huge boulder on your R to arrive at **Liqeni Madhe**, 40mins from the saddle above Liqeni i Kuçishtës.

Pass the lake on your R and ascend gradually with Guri i Kuq (2522m) on your L and the sound of a spring coming from the scree slopes, to reach a trail junction 1hr beyond Liqeni Madhe. Turn R (E) and follow the marked path up towards Qafa e Jelenkut (marked as 90mins, but it's actually only around half that). Pass a saddle with a spring below the trail on your R, to reach the **Qafa e Jelenkut** (Jelenak Pass, 2272m) with a prominent double rock outcrop below on your R.

Follow a clear path to the L of the rock outcrop and across grassy slopes, then along the top of the ridge, heading more or less S or SW. Where the ridge narrows, with the village of Roshkodol appearing in the valley below on your L, pass a prominent marked trail which branches off to the L and doubles back to the NW, towards Milishevc – which you don't take. Instead keep straight ahead (SW) along the crest of the ridge – there are no trail markings at first, but a little over 1hr from Qafa e Jelenkut you reach a small **lake** with a sign marking the way ahead along the ridge towards the Zavoj Pass (Sedlo Zavoj). There's a small level grassy area beside the lake where it would be possible to camp, but there's no spring.

Continue past the lake for another 15mins to reach another junction, from which another trail to Milishevc – the one you followed on Stage 4 – branches off to the L. Go straight ahead, retracing your route from Stage 4 in reverse, to reach the trail junction and signpost at the **Zavoj Pass** (Sedlo Zavoj, 2167m; marked on the GIZ map as Ravno Brdo) in 1hr.

View from the trail above Liqeni Madhe

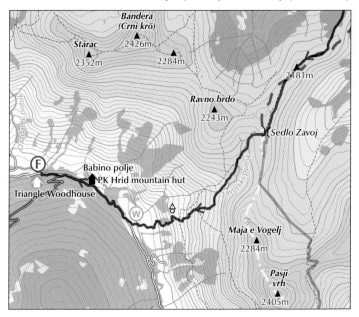

From the Zavoj Pass, turn R (W) and head downhill on a clear path across beautiful meadows covered with masses of wildflowers and blueberries. Go L over a stream, after which trail markings become very unclear: almost immediately after the loose rocky section of path that follows the stream, look for a marked path on your R – the initial marking is easily missed but markings become clear afterwards – which leads down towards a long single wooden building with a lone tree to the L of it. (The path is easily missed – in which case you can just pick your way downhill on faint livestock trails, aiming for the long wooden building and lone tree.)

Pass the **wooden building** on your R (the path goes past the lone tree to the L of this), go downhill and bear L initially, before the path goes across a small stream and downhill more steeply. Go to the R of a barbed wire fence running up the hillside from a farm building, then L at the bottom of the fence and behind the farm building, and from here down to the 4WD road.

Follow the 4WD road to the river, which you cross by a footbridge a little to the R of where the road fords the river, then rejoin the 4WD road and ascend to reach a junction and a roadside **spring** on your R, 1hr 45mins from the Zavoj Pass.

Signpost at a trail junction on the Zavoj Pass, with Marijash in the background

Continue along the 4WD road, through pine forest and passing the scattered houses of **Babino polje**. **Triangle Woodhouse** is on your L about 30mins from the roadside spring and around 2hrs from the Zavoj Pass.

BABINO POLJE

The village of Babino polje (meaning 'Grandma's fields') stretches along the valley of the Temnjačka stream, a tributary of the Lim. Mobile phone signal is very week in Babino polje. A taxi to Plav costs around €35.

Food and lodging

Triangle Woodhouse (tel +49 179 388 6101; **triangle-woodhouse.com**; food served). Wonderfully homely and welcoming guesthouse in Babino polje. Excellent English spoken, as well as German.

Gago's Wooden House (**www.booking.com/hotel/me/gagos-wooden-house. en-gb.html**; food served).

Isov Ranch (**www.booking.com/hotel/me/isov-ranch-plav1.en-gb.html**; food served).

Pinetrees Lodge (**https://lodgebetweenthepinetrees.business.site**; food served). Also called Lodge Between the Pines.

Tri-S Guesthouse (**https://tri-s-guest-house.business.site/**; food served).

PK Hrid mountain hut (pskhrid@t-com.me).

STAGE 8
Babino polje (Montenegro) – Plav (Montenegro)

Start	Babino polje (1490m, Montenegro)
Finish	Plav (968m, Montenegro)
Distance	20km
Ascent/descent	720m/1250m
Time	6hrs 30mins
Terrain	Gradual ascent on 4WD roads through forest, then good clear paths; one section of boulder-hopping near Hridsko jezero; the last parts of the route are also on 4WD roads and farm tracks, with some asphalt walking in Plav.
Highest point	2062m (Veliki Hrid)
Maps	Veliki Hrid is marked incorrectly on the GIZ map
Access	No public transport to Babino polje; a taxi (ask Armend Alija at Triangle Log Guesthouse in Babino polje) will cost around €35 from Plav.
Food and lodging	Guesthouses, campsites, hotels and restaurants in Plav
Intermediate stops	Guesthouse at Katun Bajrović (food served)

A long but straightforward stage passing the beautiful Hridsko jezero, a lake at 1972m below the jagged, rocky peaks of Veliki krš and krš Bogićevica. The stage is very well marked, having been completely re-marked in 2016.

Follow the 4WD road back uphill (E) from Triangle Woodhouse in **Babino polje**, retracing your steps from Stage 7. After 5mins turn R up a 4WD road signposted to Hridsko jezero, then 30mins later take a R fork, still along a 4WD road, to reach the first cottages of Katun Bajrović, with views of Visitor on your R and passing a **spring** on your L.

It's another 10mins along the 4WD road to **Samelova koliba**, newly opened in 2016 and situated on an open hillside with nice views, shortly before the main settlement of Katun Bajrović, just over 1hr from Babino polje. There's another **spring** here. Continue along the 4WD a further 10mins to the main settlement of **Katun Bajrović**, turn L onto a grassy 4WD track (signposted to Hridsko jezero) then almost immediately turn L up a marked path. (Don't continue straight ahead into the forest on the 4WD track: it fizzles out after 20mins.)

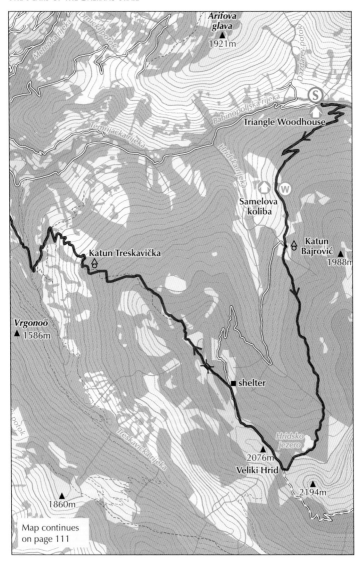

Arifova
glava
1921m

Triangle Woodhouse

Samelova
koliba

Katun Treskavička

Katun
Bajrović
1988m

Vrgonoö
1586m

shelter

Hridsko
jezero

Veliki Hrid
2076m

2194m

1860m

Map continues
on page 111

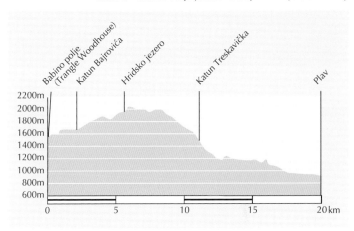

Ascend through forest, then cross a meadow and bear R across a stream, after which the path becomes steeper and rockier. Pass a small pond on your R, then bear R to reach the shore of **Hridsko jezero**, a large lake at 1972m nestled below the rocky summit of Veliki krš, 2hrs 30mins from Babino polje.

Unlike many of the other lakes on the Peaks of the Balkans Trail, Hridsko jezero (**Lake Hrid**) is deep enough that you can swim in it – although you can

Hikers brave the chilly water for a late September swim in Hridsko jezero

109

Trekkers take a break at a saddle on the trail down from Hridsko jezero

expect the water to be suitably chilly. (If you need further incentive, locals say that a swim in Hridsko jezero guarantees you a happy marriage!) You can walk around the shore of the lake, and there are plenty of level areas for a picnic.

Turn L and follow the shore of the lake, then cross some large boulders to reach a trail junction and signpost. Go straight ahead downhill (marked Veliki Hrid) then ascend to **Veliki Hrid**, a trail junction on a 4WD road at 2062m.

Turning L up this 4WD road (not on the Peaks of the Balkans Trail) would lead to Ćafa Bogićes on the border with Kosovo in 3hrs 30mins, thus providing a possible route to Tromedja and Dobërdol – see Stage 4. It also provides an approach to Veliki krš, 2374m, also known as Hridski krš or krš Bogićevica.

Turn R and follow the 4WD road downhill to reach a small, unstaffed **mountain shelter** (*sklonište*) on your R after 25mins (usually locked; owned by PK Hrid mountain club in Plav, pskhrid.webs.com). Turn L onto a marked path opposite the shelter and follow this uphill to reach a grassy **saddle** at around 2010m in 10mins, marked confusingly as Veliki Hrid on both the GIZ and Prokletije National Park maps. This makes another decent spot for a break, with good views of Visitor, the mountain on the far side of Lake Plav.

Follow the marked trail to your R from the saddle (not straight ahead downhill), then after about 5mins look for a marked path on your R through some trees leading steeply downhill. Cross a rocky gully then continue downhill to a clearing with a signpost marking Plav as 4hrs away (although it shouldn't take you much more than 3hrs).

After the clearing go L over a stream then bear L, then R and downhill, and R where the path meets a larger trail. Go R onto a 4WD then L onto a marked path again, across a meadow and bear R onto a 4WD road, with **Katun Treskavička** on your R, 4hrs 30mins from Babino polje.

Follow the 4WD road downhill, keeping straight ahead at a crossroads, to reach another 4WD road beside a river. Turn R onto this 4WD road then go L onto a marked path across a grassy area. Cross a stream, after which the path becomes a muddy farm track. Pass a succession of three springs on your L, and go downhill to reach the main asphalt road on the outskirts of **Plav** (this is the road leading towards Babino polje), 2hrs from Katun Treskavička.

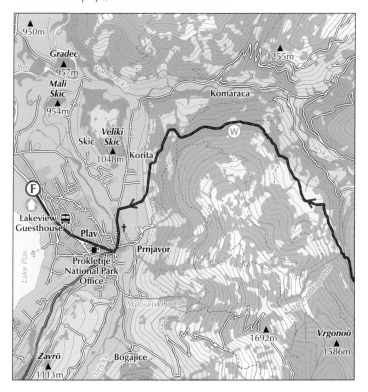

Turn L along the main road, passing the cemetery, then turn R (continuing straight ahead for less than 100m would lead you to Kula Redžepagića, a medieval fortified tower house) and follow a street (called Čaršija) uphill to the roundabout in the town centre, beside the **Prokletije National Park office**. Go straight ahead and downhill, with the lake on your L, to reach the bus station (on your R) and 30mins after reaching the main asphalt road, **LakeViews Camp and Guesthouse** (on your L).

PLAV

Plav – the only town of any size on the Peaks of the Balkans route – sits on the shore of Lake Plav, a large glacial lake at 906m. Lake Plav is fed by the River Ljuča from the northwest and drained by the River Lim, which flows on into Serbia and then Bosnia where it joins the River Drina. The lake and surrounding rivers contain several species of freshwater fish, including grayling, Danube salmon, lake trout and burbot.

There are shops and supermarkets along the road between the bus station and the roundabout. The Prokletije National Park office is on the roundabout and is open 8am–4pm Mon–Fri. Kula Redžepagića, near the National Park office, is a good example of the type of fortified tower house typical of this region, and dates from the 17th century (for more information on kulas, see the section on Theth in Stage 10). For the Border Police office, go downhill (E) from the roundabout then L (N) and follow the road out to the edge of town.

Food and lodging

LakeViews Camp and Guesthouse (tel +382 (0)67 672 683; food served). Excellent guesthouse and campsite, with very nice food – try the house specialty, *sarma* (pickled cabbage leaves stuffed with rice and mince). The owner, Vujica Martić, speaks a little English. Hands down the best (and best value) place to stay in Plav.

Emina (**www.booking.com/hotel/me/emina-plav.en-gb.html**).

Hostel Bear Hug (**www.booking.com/hotel/me/hostel-bear-hug.en-gb.html**; food served).

Eco Village Jasavić (**www.booking.com/hotel/me/seotsko-domacinstvo-jasavic.en-gb.html**; food served).

Hotel Kula Damjanova (**https://kuladamjanova.com/**; food served). More expensive and less conveniently located 2km outside Plav on the road to Gusinje, but a beautiful setting.

There is a supermarket on the road between the bus station and the National Park Office.

Transport

The bus station is a 10min walk along the main road SE of LakeViews (around five buses a day to Podgorica, as well as buses to Gusinje).

The Grbaja Valley

Anyone spending an extra day in Plav should take some time off the Trail to visit the Grbaja Valley, which runs parallel to (and just north of) the Ropojana valley, and contains some of the most spectacular mountain scenery anywhere in Montenegro. Minibuses run between Plav and Gusinje, from where it's 7km by asphalt road to reach the head of the Grbaja Valley, from where several hiking routes begin. Volušnica (1879m), a lookout point on the north side of the valley, makes for a good, straightforward hike which you can do in half a day, with jaw-dropping views of the Karanfili peaks. Start from just beyond the Dom Branko Kotlajic mountain hut on the valley floor and follow the clear trail uphill towards Volušnica, bearing left when you reach the grassy cirque (allow 4hrs return from the hut, with 720m ascent/descent). For enhanced views, continue E up the ridge to Taljanka (2057m).

Peaks at the head of the Grbaja Valley in moonlight

STAGE 9

Plav (Montenegro) –
Vusanje (Montenegro)

Start	Plav (968m, Montenegro)
Finish	Vusanje (1025m, Montenegro)
Distance	27.5km
Ascent/descent	1140m/1080m
Time	8hrs
Terrain	Long (over 10km) section along 4WD road initially, and one short section on 4WD road at the end. Clear, very well marked paths, with one short very steep section.
Highest point	2106m (Vrh Bora)
Maps	The GIZ marks Feratovića katun as Karaula Feratovića, and misplaces the route slightly southeast of Vrh Bora; it does not mark the route over the Prosllopit Pass (Stage 2), which comes within 5mins of Stage 9.
Access	No public transport to Vusanje
Food and lodging	Guesthouses and campsites in Vusanje
Intermediate stops	None. If you need to camp, there's a good level spot near a spring, at the point where this stage almost meets the route of Stage 2 below Maja Kolata and the Prosllopit Pass.

This stage begins with a long (over 10km) hike up a 4WD track to Feratovića katun – after which it becomes one of the most beautiful stages of the Peaks of the Balkans Trail, with staggering views. This stage is often skipped by guided groups and somewhat maligned due to the long road walk-in – which is a shame as you can avoid the 4WD section with a jeep transfer, and the lack of trail markings on this stage are now a thing of the past, since it was very well marked out in 2016 thanks to the efforts of Ahmet Reković. The route description on the GIZ map bears little resemblance to the route as it is now marked on the ground.

A jeep transfer to Feratovića katun (and it will need to be a jeep/4X4, as a car won't be able to get more than half way) will cost around €60 – contact Zalaz www.zalaz.me/contact-us (depending on the weather and/or road conditions, the jeep may quite likely only be able to go as far as a couple

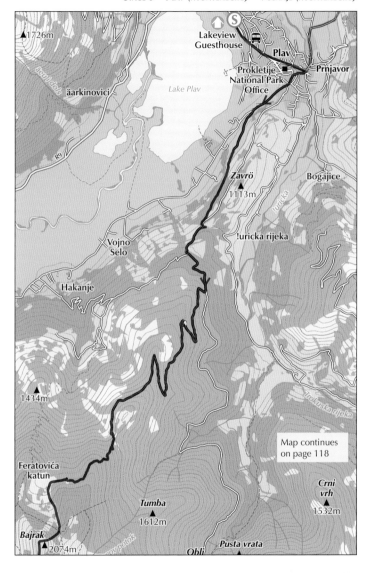

Lakeview
Guesthouse

Plav

Prnjavor

Prokletije
National Park
Office

Lake Plav

▲1726m

äarkinovici

R9

Zavrö
1113m

Bogajice

!uricka rijeka

Vojno
Selo

Hakanje

▲1434m

Trokuska rijeka

Map continues
on page 118

Feratovića
katun

Tumba
1612m

*Crni
vrh*
1532m

Bajrak
▲2074m

...oy potok

Obli

Pusta vrata

of km before Feratovića katun – after that there's an incredibly steep section which is not all that safe to drive).

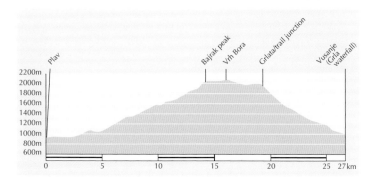

From the roundabout and the National Park office in **Plav**, follow the red and white trail markings S along the asphalt road towards Vojno selo and Gusinje, then bear L. It's 10km of gradual uphill to reach **Feratovića katun**, clearly marked the whole way and mostly through the forest – allow at least 3hrs if you're walking. Feratovića katun stands on the far edge of a large meadow, with beautiful views down over Lake Plav and across to Visitor.

Early-morning view from the trail up to Bajrak

Turn L (S) up an unmarked path beside the forest towards a saddle to the L of Bajrak. It's 20mins up to the saddle, from where a clearly marked trail branches off to the R up Bajrak, following the crest of a ridge. The path itself is faint in places, quite loose, and is extremely steep. After 25mins you reach the top of the ridge – the views back from here are breathtaking – from where a more gentle, also marked path leads in 5mins to the top of **Bajrak** (2074m). The views from Bajrak are magnificent, stretching to the wild, rocky peaks and karst badlands above the Grbaja and Ropojana valleys.

Follow the spur SSE from Bajrak to reach a clearing, turn R along the edge of this and ascend gradually to a ridge which you follow SSW to its highest point, **Vrh Bora** (2106m), 40mins from Bajrak. The views from here are an enhanced version of those from Bajrak, with Maja Kolata and the Prosllopit Pass dominant to the south, and the peaks above the Ropojana and Grbaja valleys to the west.

Follow the ridge SSE from Vrh Bora towards the Prosllopit Pass and Kolata, then along the L side of the ridge and between **two small lakes**. Where the path splits, bear R and slightly downhill below a rock outcrop, with the Prosllopit Pass still ahead. Bear R and gradually downhill, but don't take a shortcut down to the path below or double back on this. Instead keep straight ahead until just after passing a **spring** on your L, then descend and cross the remnants of a low stone wall to a prominent trail marking on the side of a rock, where you turn R. Follow the trail between two rocky areas then descend and bear R, to reach a junction with a signpost, around 45mins from Vrh Bora.

View of the peaks above the Ropojana Valley from Vrh Bora

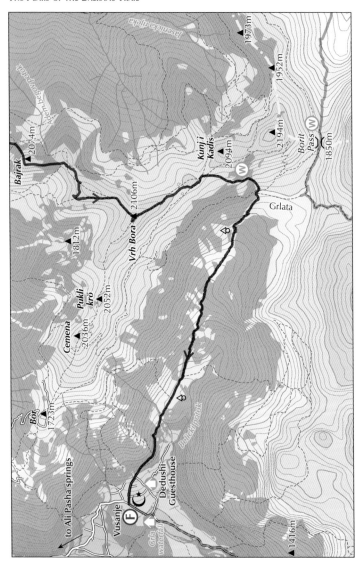

Turn R (NW, signposted to Vusanje and marked as 2hrs 30mins, but allowing 2hrs is sufficient) and follow trail markings that lead across the top of rocky karst formations. Bear R and down, cross a level meadow then descend further. Cross a gully, then a stream, and follow a braided path downhill to reach a **katun** on your R, 30mins from the signpost.

Continue across pasture then into the forest. Cross a stream, descending further and passing another **katun** on your L, where some traditional stone houses were being built in 2016. Go straight ahead onto a 4WD road, passing a small cemetery on your L, before descending with views over Vusanje and the Ropojana Valley.

Pass a trail on your L leading down to **Dedushi Guesthouse**, and continue down to reach the asphalt road beside the mosque in **Vusanje**, 2hrs 30mins from Vrh Bora. Turn L and follow the road 5mins down and over a bridge, just after which there's a small parking and picnic area on your R, beside the **Grla waterfall** and the adjacent restaurant and guesthouse, with the Ropojana Valley stretching beyond.

VUSANJE

Vusanje is a small village at the mouth of the Ropojana Valley. At the south end of the village, a stream (the Skakavica, meaning 'grasshopper') plunges down the Grla waterfall. If you have time for a short detour, it's a 1hr walk up the asphalt road (N, towards Gusinje) to Ali Pasha springs, where water gushes up out of the hillside to form a small lake.

Food and lodging

Dedushi Guesthouse (**www.booking.com/hotel/me/dedushi-guesthouse-amp-wod-cabin.en-gb.html**; food served). On the L as you descend into Vusanje.

Ulaj Guesthouse (**www.booking.com/hotel/me/guest-house-ulaj.en-gb.html**; food served).

Guesthouse Vucetaj (**https://guest-house-vucetaj.business.site/**).

Prokletije Eko Cabin Vusanje (**www.booking.com/hotel/me/vuthaj-eko-katun-vusanje-gusinje1.en-gb.html**; food served).

Riverside Guesthouse (**www.booking.com/hotel/me/riverside-guesthouse.en-gb.html**).

Bungalows Oaza (**www.booking.com/hotel/me/bungalows-oaza.en-gb.html**).

Guesthouse Kollata (**www.booking.com/hotel/me/guest-house-kollata-vusanje.en-gb.html**; food served).

STAGE 10
Vusanje (Montenegro) – Theth (Albania)

Start	Vusanje (1025m, Montenegro)
Finish	Theth (728m, Albania)
Distance	21.3km
Ascent/descent	1110m/1440m
Time	7hrs 30mins
Terrain	4WD roads along the Ropojana Valley and at the end of the stage, approaching Theth; good paths in between, mostly well marked; the long descent from the Pejë Pass (Qafa e Pejës) into the Theth Valley is on a well-engineered mule track, quite broad but exposed on one side.
Highest point	1707m (Qafa e Pejës)
Maps	Theth is also written 'Thethi'
Access	No public transport to either Vusanje or Theth
Food and lodging	Plenty of guesthouses and campsites in Theth
Intermediate stops	Guesthouses at Okoli

This stage – one of the finest on the Peaks of the Balkans Trail – follows the beautiful Ropojana Valley before climbing past a seasonal lake to the Pejë Pass (Qafa e Pejës) and descending into the Theth Valley in Albania. Water can be collected from a spring at Fusha e Ruinicës.

When the English traveller **Edith Durham** visited this area in the early 1900s, crossing the border from Albania and following the Ropojana Valley towards Vusanje and Gusinje (a journey she published as *High Albania* in 1908), this then-corner of the Ottoman Empire was so closed to foreigners that she had to travel in disguise, and famously described Gusinje as 'the Lhasa of Europe'.

From the picnic area beside the Grla waterfall in **Vusanje**, follow the 4WD SW along the Ropojana Valley. Around 20mins from the picnic area a path on your R leads down in 2mins to an intense blue-green pool, known as **Oko Skakavice** (*oko* means eye), where the stream (the Skakavica, meaning 'grasshopper') rises from a spring.

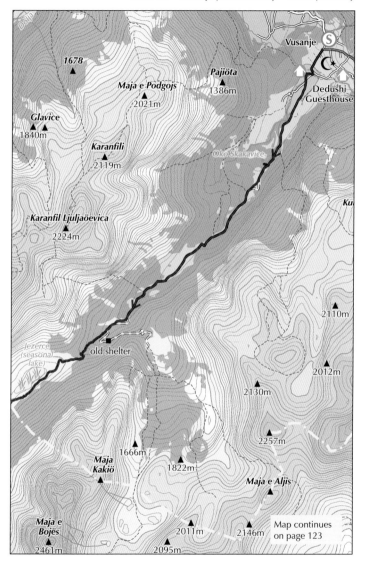

Vusanje S

Dedushi
Guesthouse

1678

Maja e Podgojs
2021m

Pajiöta
1386m

Glavice
1840m

Karanfili
2119m

Oko Skakavice

Ku

Karanfil Ljuljaöevica
2224m

2110m

Jezerce
(seasonal
lake)

old shelter

2012m

2130m

2257m

Maja Kakiö

1666m

1822m

Maja e Aljis

Maja e Bojës
2461m

2011m

2095m

2146m

Map continues
on page 123

121

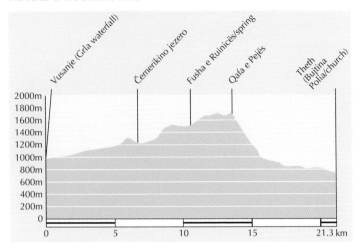

Return to the 4WD track, turn R and continue along the Ropojana Valley, with the scree gullies leading up to the Karanfili peaks (which can be climbed from the Grbaja Valley) on your R, and some wildly impressive crags on your L, leading up towards Maja Rosit and the Albanian border.

One prominent crag, visible around 90mins from the picnic area, is called **Đevojka** ('girl') – named, according to local legend, after a young woman who threw herself from the summit.

Around 1hr 45mins from picnic area, turn R off the 4WD onto a marked path which leads gradually uphill through bushes and low trees to reach an open grassy area in 30mins. (If you continue a few minutes further along the 4WD, a track on the L leads to Zastan, a ruined military barracks and possible campsite, from where trails lead to Maja Rosit and Maja Jezerces.)

Ahead of you is a lake bed – Čemerikino jezero (or just **Jezerce**) in Montenegrin, Liqeni Geshtares in Albanian – usually dry as it is only fed by snow melt, although there's a chance you may find some water here early in the season. The Montenegrin Border Police sometimes have a jeep parked above the near shore of the lake, and may ask to check your cross-border permit. Go straight ahead across the lake bed, following a clear path close to the L side. When you reach the far side of the lake bed, you're in Albania – the border is marked by a small concrete pyramid.

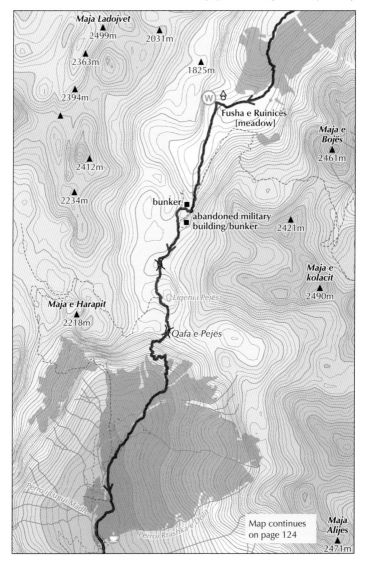

Map continues
on page 124

From here the path zigzags up through forest to reach **Fusha e Ruinicës**, a meadow with plenty of level areas for camping, although livestock is usually grazed here. At the far end of the meadow below a rock outcrop there are a couple of shepherd huts, and just above these a **spring** with water channelled into a trough.

Turn L (S) from the shepherd huts following a clear path across level grassland, with a ravine appearing on your R. Ascend gradually, passing an old concrete military **bunker** then bearing R and crossing the stream.

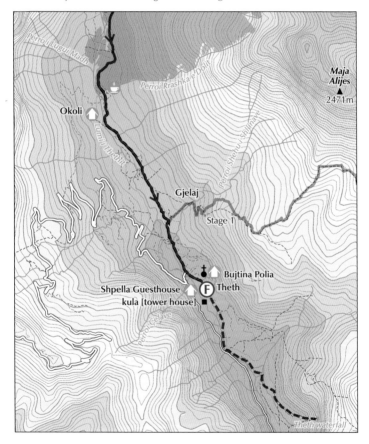

Crags above the Ropojana Valley

Albania's former Communist leader Enver Hoxha had around half a million of these little **bunkers** – many of which still remain – built in almost any conceivable location across the country between 1967 and 1986, to defend the country against any possible invasion, something which never came.

Keep ascending above another bunker (told you there were lots!) to reach a **saddle**. The way from here is less clear at first – don't follow the more obvious path on your R (signposted Lepush); instead go straight ahead and slightly L of a group of stone-walled enclosures, and ascend aiming for an obvious notch. The prominent peak on the right is Maja Harapit. Once you reach the notch the way ahead is clear – down past a small lake, **Liqeni i Pejës**, which is surrounded by enormous blocks of rock, then up steadily to the pass, **Qafa e Pejës** (Pejë Pass, 1707m), 4hrs after leaving the 4WD track in the Ropojana Valley.

Below the dizzying south face of Maja Harapit is Albania's longest known **cave** (suitable only for experienced and suitably equipped cavers), stretching horizontally some 2585m and including a whopping 320m drop at one point. The cave entrances are located just above the edge of the forest at the north end of the Theth Valley.

A trail on the R leads from just N of the Pejë Pass (near Liqeni i Pejës, before the final climb to the pass) to **Maja Harapit** (2218m, also written Maja e Arapit or Maja e Harapit). The plateau on the N side of the summit

125

Peaks above the Pejë Pass

pyramid has pronounced karst formations – limestone pavement, vertical fissures, and so on. Maja Harapit's striking, pointy summit itself is surrounded by steep cliffs – and the S face is a giddying 800m sheer drop. (The E buttress does provide a reasonably accessible, non-technical route up to the summit, for confident scramblers – although it is still extremely exposed in places.)

From Qafa e Pejës head downhill towards the Theth Valley on a clear path past a group of crosses, above, and then below, some stupendous cliffs (there's a sheer drop on the R of the trail).

On reaching a 4WD track follow this downhill, passing a small makeshift café/bar on your left, 90mins below Qafa e Pejës. After a further 15mins bear R downhill where the 4WD road forks, then follow the 4WD road as it bears L, passing the village of **Okoli** on your R, where there are several guesthouses. Don't go R over the bridge but keep straight ahead along the 4WD road lined by plum trees, passing a series of guesthouses and campsites, following the signs to the *kisha* (church) then after the church comes into view bearing L where the road forks. **Bujtina Polia** (Polia Guesthouse) is just after the church on your R.

THETH

Kula (defensive tower house) in Theth

Theth is a predominantly Catholic village near the head of the Theth Valley, towered over by the south face of Maja Harapit and other surrounding peaks. Theth's church was built in 1892, and in 1917 the first school to teach in the Albanian language was opened in Theth, by the Catholic priest Shtjefen Gjeçovi.

Theth also has the best example of a fortified medieval tower house or *kula* along the route of the Peaks of the Balkans Trail. The Nicoll Kolçeku Kula is located just south of Bujtina Polia and Shpella guesthouse, on an outcrop of limestone, and dates from the 17th century. These distinctive tower houses, once common across northern Albania, provided refuge during conflicts, including when someone had committed murder. According to the laws on blood feud, laid out in the *Kanun of Leke Dukagjini*, a person could stay safely inside a kula for two weeks while local elders heard and evaluated the circumstances of the murder, and attempted to reconcile differences with the victim's relatives and pay blood money. Entry cost €1 in 2016.

There are some nice excursions around Theth – see the short Theth waterfall excursion below. For a longer day out, you can visit the 'Blue Eye', a bright blue pool fed by a spring, west of the village.

Food and lodging

Bujtina Polia (tel +355 (0)67 526 7526 or +355 (0)66 666 9944; food served). Wonderful guesthouse with lovely, welcoming hosts and heavenly food. The owner, Pavlin Polia, was involved in marking out trails in the area and spear-heading sustainable tourism in Theth when the Peaks of the Balkans Trail was being developed.

Shpella Guesthouse (tel +355 (0)69 377 4851; **www.booking. com/544379f048e939**; food served). Near the kula.

Guesthouse Pashko (**www.booking.com/hotel/al/guesthouse-pashko.en-gb. html**; food served). 200m SE of the church.

Villa Gjeçaj (**https://villagjecaj.com/our-rooms/**; food served). Near the road bridge.

Bujtina Leke Gerla (www.booking.com/hotel/al/bujtina-leke-gerla.en-gb.html; food served). 50M SW of Bujtina Polja.

Bujtina Kometa (www.booking.com/hotel/al/bujtina-kometa.en-gb.html; food served). Okol.

Kulla e Sadri Lukes (www.booking.com/hotel/al/kullat-e-sadri-lukes.en-gb.html; food served). Okol.

Info

For more information on Theth and its surroundings, see **thethi-guide.com**.

Transport

During summer there's a minibus from Theth to Shkodër. A taxi to Tirana costs around €120.

Theth waterfall excursion

This is a short, easy excursion (6km return, with 190m of ascent/descent) and is worthwhile doing regardless of whether or not you are spending an extra day in Theth. Behind **Bujtina Polia**, go L along a path beside fields, passing **Shpella Guesthouse** on your R. Pass the old stone *kula* (tower) on your L then go downhill towards the river and cross the red steel and wooden footbridge (wobbly in 2016). Follow the broad track on the far side of the bridge, then bear L and follow a path beside an irrigation channel, then climb steeply up a path to reach the **Theth waterfall** (also known as the Grunas waterfall), which tumbles around 34m into a greenish pool. Return by the same route. Allow 45mins each way.

Theth waterfall

APPENDIX A
Useful contacts

Embassies and consulates

British Embassies
In Albania

Rruga Skenderbeg 12
Tirana
tel +355 (0)4 223 4973/4/5
www.gov.uk (search 'Tirana')

In Kosovo

Lidhja e Pejes 177
Pristina
tel +381 (0)38 254 700
www.gov.uk (search 'Pristina')

In Montenegro

Ulcinjska 8, Gorica C
81000 Podgorica
tel +382 (0)20 618 010
www.gov.uk (search 'Podgorica')

Netherlands Embassies
In Albania

Rruga Asim Zeneli 10
Tirana
tel +355 (0)4 2240 828
www.netherlandsworldwide.nl

In Kosovo

Xhemajl Berisha 12
Velania
Pristina
tel +381 (0)38 516 101
www.netherlandsworldwide.nl

In Montenegro

There is no Netherlands Embassy in Montenegro, but there is one in Belgrade (Serbia):

Simina 29
Belgrade
Serbia
tel +381 (0)11 202 3900
www.netherlandsworldwide.nl

French Embassies
In Albania

Rruga Skënderbej 14
Tirana
tel +355 (0)4 238 9700
www.ambafrance-al.org

In Kosovo

Ismail Qemali 67
Dragodan
Pristina
tel +381 (0)38 2245 8800
www.ambafrance-kosovo.org

In Montenegro

Atinska 35
Podgorica
tel +382 (0)20 655 348
www.ambafrance-me.org

German Embassies
In Albania

Rruga Skënderbej 8
Tirana
tel +355 (0)4 2274 505
www.tirana.diplo.de

In Kosovo

Azem Jashanica 17
Dragodan
Pristina
tel +381 (0)38 254 500
www.pristina.diplo.de

In Montenegro
Hercegovačka 10
Podgorica
tel +382 (0)20 441 000
www.podgorica.diplo.de

US Embassies
In Albania
Rruga e Elbasanit 103
Tirana
tel +355 (0)4 2247 285
https://al.usembassy.gov/

In Kosovo
Nazim Hikmet 30
Dragodan
Pristina
tel +381 (0)38 5959 3000
https://xk.usembassy.gov/

In Montenegro
Dzona Dzeksona 2
81000 Podgorica
tel +382 (0)20 410 500
https://me.usembassy.gov/

Maps and books
Daunt (UK)
www.dauntbooks.co.uk

Stanfords (UK)
www.stanfords.co.uk

The Map Shop (the best selection of maps and guidebooks in the UK)
www.themapshop.co.uk

Mountaineering associations and mountain rescue
Mountaineering Association of Montenegro
www.pscg.me

Mountain Rescue Montenegro
www.gss-cg.me

Local tour operators

The most experienced tour operators for Peaks of the Balkans (they were both directly involved in setting up the Trail) are Zbulo and Zalaz:
Zbulo
tel +355 (0)69 2121 612 or
+355 (0)69 6731 932
email welcome@zbulo.org
zbulo.org

Zalaztel +382 (0)69 314 222
email welcome@zalaz.me
www.zalaz.me

Outdoor Kosovo
tel +44 (0)7801 947007 or +386 (0)49 168 566
outdoorkosova.com

Balkan Natural Adventure
tel +383 (0)49 661 105
www.bnadventure.com

Kosova Outdoor
tel +383 (0)44 350 511
www.kosovaoutdoor.com

Undiscovered Montenegro
www.undiscoveredmontenegro.com

Black Mountain
www.montenegroholiday.com

Regional info
Peaks of the Balkans
www.peaksofthebalkans.com

Balkan Insight
www.balkaninsight.com

Balkan Investigative Reporting Network
birn.eu.com

Balkans Peace Park Project
www.balkanspeacepark.org

Dinarsko gorje
www.dinarskogorje.com

(Very detailed information on the
Dinaric Alps, including various peaks/
groups within Prokletije. Go to the
Planine tab, select B – Središnji pojas
Dinarskog gorja, then click on Površi
i brda Crne Gore i Prokletije. In
Montenegrin, but includes a useful
summary in English.)

Albania
Albanian National Tourist Board
www.albania.al

Journey to Valbona
www.journeytovalbona.com

Ministry of Foreign Affairs
www.punetejashtme.gov.al

Mountain Bike Albania
www.mtb.al

Thethi Guide
thethi-guide.com

TOKA (The Organisation to Conserve
the Albanian Alps)
toka-albania.org

Kosovo
ERA Group (local NGO in Pejë)
www.facebook.com/eragroup

Kosovo National Tourist Board
beinkosovo.com

Ministry of Foreign Affairs
www.mfa-ks.net

Pejë Tourist Office
www.pejatourism.org

Montenegro
Ministry of Foreign Affairs and European
Integration
www.mvpei.gov.me

Montenegro National Tourist Board
www.montenegro.travel

Montenegrin National Parks
www.nparkovi.meMountaineering
Association of Montenegro
www.pscg.me

Pedalj (best source of information for
mountain biking in Montenegro, with
maps, route profiles and GPS routes)
www.pedalaj.me

Plav Tourist Board
www.toplav.me

Podgorica Tourist Board
www.podgorica.travel

Weather forecasts in Montenegro
www.meteo.co.me

Transport

Albania
Tirana Airport
www.tirana-airport.com

Lake Koman ferries
www.komanlake.org

Kosovo
Pristina Airport (Adem Jashari)
www.airportpristina.com

Airport taxi
www.taxibeki.net

Montenegro
Podgorica Airport (Golubovci)
www.montenegroairports.com

Airport taxi
www.taxi-travel.me

Montenegrin Railways
www.zcg-prevoz.me

Podgorica Bus Station
www.busterminal.me

APPENDIX B
Accommodation

Gateway towns

Pejë (Kosovo)
Hotel Çardak
Mbretëresha Teutë 101, Pejë
tel +383 44 159 011
www.facebook.com/hotelcardak/

Pristina (Kosovo)
Hotel Prima
Lidhja e prizrenit 24, Pristina
www.booking.com/hotel/xk/prima.
de.html

Hostel Prishtina Backpackers
6 Haxhi Zeka, Pristina
www.booking.com/hotel/xk/prishtina-
backpackers.en-gb.htmll

Podgorica (Montenegro)
Hotel Terminus
Bulevar Mitra Bakića bb, Podgorica
tel +382 (0)20 622 003
www.booking.com/hotel/me/terminus-
hotel-podgorica.en-gb.html

Tirana (Albania)
Hotel Oresti Centre
Rruga Bardhok Biba, Tirana
tel +355 (0)68 202 2313
www.booking.com/hotel/al/center-
rooms-oresti.en-gb.html

The following selection of accommodation providers is not exhaustive; there are other options available, particularly in Theth and Valbona. For directions to guesthouses and other details see route description.

Stage 1

Theth
Bujtina Leke Gerla
tel +355 68 230 1955
www.booking.com/hotel/al/bujtina-
leke-gerla.en-gb.html

Bujtina Polia (food served)
tel +355 (0)67 526 7526 or
+355 (0)66 666 9944
https://bujtinapolia.com

Guesthouse Pashko (food served)
tel +355 68 278 5057
www.booking.com/hotel/al/guesthouse-
pashko.en-gb.html

Shpella Guesthouse (food served)
tel +355 (0)69 377 4851
www.booking.com/544379f048e939

Villa Gjecaj (food served)
tel +355 (0)69 601 5771
https://villagjecaj.com

Rragrami
Fusha e Gjes Hotel (food served)
tel +355 (0)67 201 8005
www.facebook.com/Hotel-Fusha-e-
Gjese-Valbone-478953032230227

Valbona
Bujtina Ahmetaj (food served)
tel +355 (0)67 322 9613
www.booking.com/hotel/al/bujtina-
ahmetaj.en-gb.html

Bujtina Brahim Selimaj (food served)
www.booking.com/hotel/al/bujtina-
brahim-selimaj.html

Guesthouse Mehmeti (food served)
tel +355 (0)68 506 8105
www.booking.com/hotel/al/guesthouse-mehmeti.en-gb.html

Kelmend Selimaj Guesthouse (food served)
tel +355 (0)67 309 3406

Rilindja Guesthouse (food served)
tel +355 (0)67 301 4638
www.journeytovalbona.com

Villas Jezerca (food served)
www.booking.com/hotel/al/villas-jezerca.en-gb.html

Stage 2

Çeremi

Altin Isufaj Guesthouse
ernestoisufaj09@gmail.com

Demi & Ernsto Isufi Guesthouse
tel +355 (0)69 411 1899 or +355 (0)68 221 5312

Guesthouse Afrimi
tel +355 (0)68 2595 358

Kujtim Gocaj Guesthouse (food served)
tel +355 (0)69 411 2739
Welcoming guesthouse, excellent food.

Relax Guesthouse (food served)
tel +383 (0)49 498 137

Vita Guesthouse (food served)
www.booking.com/hotel/al/vita-guesthouse-bajram-curri.html

Stage 3

Dobërdol

Bashkimi Guesthouse (food served)
tel +355 (0)67 456 1169

Bilbil Vatnika Guesthouse (food served)
tel +355 (0)69 789 6370
www.facebook.com/peaks.of.alps
Hot showers available

Bujtina Leonard (food served)
www.facebook.com/BUJTINALEONARD/

Dobërdol mountain hut
Basic hut; sheet sleeping bag required.

Sali Vatnikaj Guesthouse
tel +355 (0)68 3854 030

Sokol Avdiaj Guesthouse (food served)
tel +355 (0)68 3762 668
www.facebook.com/g.h.sokol.avdia?ref=hl

Stage 4

Bjeshka e Zllonopojes

Guesthouse Lojza (food served)
tel +386 (0)49 850 857 (limited signal)
www.facebook.com/GuesthouseLOJZA

Milishevc

Chalet Rusta Guesthouse (food served)
tel +377 (0)44 31 29 02, (limited mobile signal)
Adriatik_72@hotmail.com

Isuf Mehmetaj Guesthouse
tel +377 (0)44 178 758 or +377 (0)44 735 545

Kulla Guesthouse (food served)
tel +383 (0)44 261 583
https://kullaguesthouse.com

Stage 5

Rugova Valley

Rugova Camp Hotel (food served)
tel +386 (0)49 688 500
www.airbnb.co.uk – 'Rugova Camp'

Rekë e Allagës

Ariu (Mustafa) Guesthouse (food served)
tel +386 (0)49 867 098

Hostel Panorama (food served)
tel +386 (0)49 250 124
www.booking.com/hotel/xk/peaks-of-
the-balkans-trail-192-km.en-gb.html

Pushimorja Hajla
https://hajla.al/

Vilat N'MAL
tel +386 (0)49 300 029
nmal.info/

Stage 6

Drelaj
Guesthouse Bujtina Kaçaku (food
served)
tel +383 48 142 758
www.facebook.com/profile.
php?id=100075840322408

Peace House Rugove
tel +377 (0)44 223 437
www.facebook.com/pg/
PeaceHouseRugove/

Shquiponja Guesthouse (food served)tel
+386 (0)49 586 740

Villa Lulzim Lajqi
tel +386 (0)49 574 321

Liqenat i Kuçishtë
Hotel Gur i Kuq (food served)
tel +386 (0)49 150 551

Hotel and Restaurant Te Liqeni (food
served)
tel +383 (0)49 828 834
www.booking.com/hotel/xk/villa-te-
liqeni-deluxe.en-gb.html

Stage 7

Babino polje
Gago's Wooden House (food served)

www.booking.com/hotel/me/gagos-
wooden-house.en-gb.html

Gradine Katun Kamp
www.booking.com/hotel/me/gradine-
katun-kamp.en-gb.html

Isov Ranch (food served)
www.booking.com/hotel/me/isov-ranch-
plav1.en-gb.html

Pine Trees Lodge (Lodge Between the
Pine Trees)
tel +31 (0)68 485 3013 or +34 (0)68
401 7001
https://lodgebetweenthepinetrees.
business.site

PK Hrid mountain hut
email pskhrid@t-com.me

Triangle Woodhouse (food served)
tel +382 (0)49 179 388 6101
triangle-woodhouse.com

Tri-S Guesthouse
tel +382 (0)69 693 499
https://tri-s-guest-house.business.site/

Stage 8

Katun Bajrović
Samelova koliba (food served)
tel +382 (0)69 584 730
email samelovakolibahrid@gmail.com

Plav

LakeViews Camp and Guesthouse (food
served)
tel +382 (0)68 064 964
www.booking.com/hotel/me/lakeviews.
en-gb.html

Eco Village Jasavić (food served)
www.booking.com/hotel/me/seotsko-
domacinstvo-jasavic.en-gb.html

Emina
www.booking.com/hotel/me/emina-
plav.en-gb.html

Hostel Bear Hug (food served)
www.booking.com/hotel/me/hostel-bear-hug.en-gb.html

Hotel Kula Damjanova (food served)
www.kuladamjanova.com

Stage 9

Vusanje

Bungalows Oaza
www.booking.com/hotel/me/bungalows-oaza.en-gb.html

Dedushi Guesthouse (food served)
www.booking.com/hotel/me/dedushi-guesthouse-amp-wod-cabin.en-gb.html

Guesthouse Kollata (food served)
www.booking.com/hotel/me/guest-house-kollata-vusanje.en-gb.html

Guesthouse Vucetaj (food served)
tel +382 (0)69 503 079
guest-house-vucetaj.business.site/

Prokletije Eko Cabin Vusanje (food served)
www.booking.com/hotel/me/vuthaj-eko-katun-vusanje-gusinje1.en-gb.html

Restaurant Hartini
www.facebook.com/kelmend.vuthaj

Riverside Guesthouse
www.booking.com/hotel/me/riverside-guesthouse.en-gb.html

Ulaj Guesthouse (food served)
www.booking.com/hotel/me/guest-house-ulaj.en-gb.html

Stage 10

Okoli

Bujtina Kometa (food served)
tel +355 (0)68 247 2458
www.booking.com/hotel/al/bujtina-kometa.en-gb.html

Kulla Sadri Lukës Guesthouse (food served)
tel +355 (0)69 293 1107
www.booking.com/hotel/al/kullat-e-sadri-lukes.en-gb.html

Theth

For accommodation in Theth, see Stage 1, above.

APPENDIX C
Further reading

Walking guidebooks

Rudolf Abraham, *The Mountains of Montenegro* (2nd edition; Cicerone, 2015) Includes hikes in the Grbaja Valley and on Visitor.

Rudolf Abraham, *The Islands of Croatia* (Cicerone, 2014) For those combining a hike on the Peaks of the Balkans Trail with a visit to the Croatian coast.

Christian Zindel & Barbara Hausammann, *Nordalbanien Wanderführer: Thethi und Kelmend* (Huber Verlag, 2009) Detailed coverage of hiking routes inthe Theth area.

General guidebooks

Rudolf Abraham, *Montenegro: The Berlitz Pocket Guide* (Insight, 2016)

Rudolf Abraham, *National Geographic Traveller Croatia* (2nd edition; National Geographic, 2015)

Gillian Gloyer, *Albania: The Bradt Travel Guide* (7th edition; Bradt, 2022)

Gail Warrander & Verena Knaus, *Kosovo: The Bradt Travel Guide* (2nd edition; Bradt, 2010)

History and culture

Florin Curta, *Southeastern Europe in the Middle Ages 500–1250* (Cambridge, 2006)

Blendi Fevziu, *Enver Hoxha: The Iron Fist of Albania* (I.B. Tauris, 2016)

Olivier Gilkes, *Albania: An Archaeological Guide* (I.B. Tauris, 2012)

Misha Glenny, *The Fall of Yugoslavia* (London, 1992)

Tim Judah, *Kosovo: What Everyone Needs to Know* (OUP, 2008)

Noel Malcolm, *Kosovo: A Short History* (Pan, 2002)

Dimitri Obolenski, *The Byzantine Commonwealth: Eastern Europe, 500–1453* (London, 1971)

Elizabeth Roberts, *Realm of the Black Mountain* (Hurst, 2007)

Laura Silber and Allan Little, *The Death of Yugoslavia* (London, 1995) The best account of the war in the former Yugoslavia.

Miranda Vickers, *The Albanians: A Modern History* (I.B. Tauris, 2014)

Clarissa De Waal, *Albania: Portrait of a Country in Transition* (I.B. Tauris, 2013)

John Wilkes, *The Illyrians* (Oxford, 1992)

Antonia Young, *Women Who Became Men* (Bloomsbury 3PL, 2001)

Natural history

E. Nicolas Arnold and Denys W. Ovenden, *Reptiles and Amphibians of Europe* (Princeton Field Guides, 2002) reprinted from the second edition of *Collins Field Guide to the Reptiles and Amphibians of Britain and Europe* (Harper Collins, 2002)

Collins' Birds of Britain and Europe Field Guide (Harper Collins, 2004)

Klaas-Douwe B Dijkstra and Richard Lewington, *Field Guide to the Dragonflies of Britain and Europe* (British Wildlife Publishing, 2006)

Gerard Gorman, *Central and Eastern European Wildlife* (Bradt, 2008)

Gerard Gorman, *Birding in Eastern Europe* (Wildsounds, 2006)

Oleg Polunin, *Flowers of Greece and the Balkans: A Field Guide* (Oxford, 1987)

Oleg Polunin, *The Concise Flowers of Europe* (Oxford, 1972)

Lars Svensson, Peter J. Grant, Killian Mullarney and Dan Zetterström, *Birds of Europe* (Princeton University Press, 1999)

Tom Tolman and Richard Lewington, *Collins Butterfly Guide* (Collins, 2009)

Language

Linda Mëniku and Héctor Campos, *Colloquial Albanian* (Routledge, 2015)

David Norris, *Teach Yourself Serbian* (Teach Yourself, 2003)

Ramazan John Hysa, *Albanian–English Dictionary and Phrasebook* (Hippocrene, 2000)

Literature

Robert Carver, *The Accursed Mountains* (Flamingo, 2009)

Edith Durham, *High Albania* (Edward Arnold 1909; various reprints)

Robin Hanbury-Tenison, *Land of Eagles: Riding Through Europe's Forgotten Country* (I.B. Tauris, 2013)

Ismail Kadare, *Broken April* (Vintage, 2003)

Ismail Kadare, *Three Elegies for Kosovo* (Vintage, 2011)

Edward Lear, *Journeys of a Landscape Painter in Greece and the Levant* (Richard Bentley, 1852; rep. Pimlico/The Century Travellers, 1988)

Anne Pennington & Peter Levi (trans.), *Marko the Prince* (London, 1984)

APPENDIX D
Language and glossary

You will encounter both Montenegrin and Albanian while hiking the Peaks of the Balkans Trail, in Montenegro and Albania/Kosovo respectively. The following section lists the alphabets of the two languages and their pronunciation, followed by a tri-lingual glossary (English/Albanian/Montenegrin) of useful words and phrases. Both languages are phonetic, that is, every letter is always pronounced, and each letter is always pronounced the same (unlike English); and in both languages (and again, unlike in English), nouns are modified according to cases (nominative, dative, accusative etc) depending on how they are used in a sentence (although this should be perfectly familiar to anyone who has learned German, Russian or many other languages which also use cases).

Montenegrin pronunciation

Both the Latin and Cyrillic scripts are used in Montenegro – the complete alphabet in Montenegrin/Serbian has 30 letters and is given below, in both scripts. Note that a number of letters, although they appear quite familiar (in both Cyrillic and Latin scripts), are nevertheless pronounced very differently to how they would be in English: the Cyrillic letters X, J, H, P, C, Y, and B are pronounced 'h', 'y', 'n', 'r', 's', 'oo', and 'v' respectively; the Latin letters C and J are pronounced 'ts' and 'y' respectively. The following letters do not appear in the Montenegrin alphabet: q, w, x, y.

Latin	Cyrillic	Equivalent sound in English
A	Аа	as the 'a' in father
B	Бб	b
C	Цц	as the 'ts' in cats
Č	Чч	as the 'ch' in church
Ć	Ћћ	similar to č, but softer, as the 'tj' sound in picture
D	Дд	d
Đ d	Ђђ	very similar to the following letter...
Dž	Џџ	as the 'j' in jam

138

Latin	Cyrillic	Equivalent sound in English
E	Ее	as the 'e' in egg
F	Фф	f
G	Гг	pronounced hard, as the 'g' in give
H	Хх	h
I	Ии	as the 'i' in ill
J	Јј	as the 'y' in yes
K	Кк	k
L	Лл	l
Lj	Љљ	as the 'lli' in million
M	Мм	m
N	Нн	n
Nj	Њњ	as the 'ni' in onion
O	Оо	as the 'o' in hot
P	Пп	p
R	Рр	rolled slightly
S	Сс	s
Š	Шш	as the 'sh' in shake
T	Тт	as the 't' in time
U	Уу	as the 'oo' in pool
V	Вв	v
Z	Зз	as the 'z' in zoo
Ž	Жж	as the 's' in pleasure, and the French 'j' in janvier

Albanian pronunciation

There are 36 letters in the Albanian alphabet, which is listed below. As with Montenegrin, some letters, although they appear quite familiar, are pronounced quite differently to how they would be in English: the letters C, J, Q, X, and Y are pronounced 'ts', 'y', 'ch', 'ds' and 'oo' respectively.

Latin	Equivalent sound in English
A	as the 'a' in car
B	as the 'b' in big
C	as the 'ts' in cats
Ç	as the initial 'ch' in church
D	as the 'd' in dog
Dh	as the 'th' in there
E	as the 'e' in get
Ë	as the 'u' in hurt
F	as the 'f' in free
G	pronounced hard, as the 'g' in get
Gj	as the 'dg' in judge
I	as the 'ee' in see
J	as the 'y' in yes
K	as the 'k' in kite
L	as the 'l' in log
Ll	as a double 'l', as in ball
M	as the 'm' in mat
N	as the 'n' in not
Nj	as the 'n' in news, and the 'ni' in onion
O	as the 'o' in hot
P	as the 'p' in pat
Q	pronounced as a soft 'ch', as the 't' in mature
R	as the 'r' in road
Rr	as a rolled 'r'
S	as the 's' in sun
Sh	as the 'sh' in sheep
T	as the 't' in tin
Th	as the 'th' in thin

Latin	Equivalent sound in English
U	as the 'u' in put
V	as the 'v' in very
X	as the 'ds' in kids
Xh	as the 'j' in jam
Y	as the 'u' ('oo') in the French word tu
Z	as the 'z' in zoo
Zh	as the 's' in pleasure, and the French 'j' in janvier

Glossary of useful words and phrases

Greetings

English	Albanian	Montenegrin
Hello/Good day	Përshëndetje	Dobar dan
Hi/bye! (informal)	Tungatjeta!	Zdravo! or Ćao! (pronounced as Italian 'ciao')
Good morning	Mirëmëngjes	Dobro jutro
Good evening	Mirëmbrëma	Dobro veče
Goodbye	Mirupafshim	Do viđenja
How are you?	Si jeni?	Kako ste?
Fine, thank you	Mirë, falemenderit	Dobro, hvala
Pleased to meet you	Gëzohem	Drago mi je
Where are you from?	Nga jeni?	Odakle ste?
I'm from... (England/ Scotland/Ireland/ Wales/Germany)	Jam nga... (Anglia/ Scocia/Irlanda/Uells/ Gjermania)	Ja sam iz... (Engleska/ Škotska/Irska/Vels/ Njemačka)

Basics

English	Albanian	Montenegrin
Yes	Po	Da
No	Jo	Ne
Please	Ju lutem	Molim
Thank you	Faleminderit	Hvala

English	Albanian	Montenegrin
You're welcome	S'ka përse	Molim/Nema na čemu
Bon apetit!	T'bëftë mirë!	Prijatno!
Cheers!	Gëzuar!	Živjeli!
Excuse me/Sorry	Me falni	Izvinite/Oprostite
Please could I have...	Unë dua...	Molim vas...
Do you have...?	A keni...?	Da li imate...?
How much does it cost?	Sa kushton?	Koliko košta?
Where is...?	Ku është...?	Gdje je...?
good/bad	mire/keq	dobro/loše
today	sot	danas
tomorrow	dje	sutra
morning	mëngjes	ujutro
evening	mbrëmbje	naveče

Language difficulties

English	Albanian	Montenegrin
Do you speak English/French/German?	A flisni Anglisht/Frengjisht/Gjermanisht?	Da li govorite engleski/francuski/njemački?
I don't understand	S'kuptoj	Ne razumijem

Accommodation

English	Albanian	Montenegrin
Do you have a room?	A keni një dhomë?	Da li imate sobu?
half-board	gjysem pension	polu pansion
toilet (men/women)	banjo (burrat/gratë)	toalet (za muškarce/za žene)
shower	dush	tuš

Food and drink

English	Albanian	Montenegrin
restaurant	*restorant*	*restoran*
menu	*menu*	*meni*
breakfast	*mëngjesi*	*doručak*
lunch	*dreka*	*ručak*
dinner	*darka*	*večera*
I'm vegetarian	*Unë jam vegjetarian*	*Ja sam vegetarijanac (m)/vegetarijaka (f)*
apple	*mollë*	*jabuka*
beer	*birrë*	*pivo*
bread	*bukë*	*hljeb*
cheese	*djathë*	*sir*
coffee (Turkish)	*kafe (Turke)*	*(turska) kafa*
dessert	*ëmbëlsirë*	*desert*
fish	*peshk*	*riba*
fruit	*pemë*	*voće*
meat	*mish*	*meso*
milk	*qumësht*	*mlijeko*
pasta	*makarona*	*tjestenina*
salad	*sallatë*	*salata*
soup	*supë*	*čorba*
sugar	*sheqer*	*šećer*
tea	*çaj*	*čaj*
trout	*troftë*	*pastrmka*
vegetables	*perime*	*povrće*
water	*ujë*	*voda*

Transport

English	Albanian	Montenegrin
bicycle	biçikletë	bicikl
bus	autobus	avtobus
bus station	stacioni i autobusëve	autobuska stanica
bus stop	stacion autobusi	stanica
car	veturë	kola
ferry	target	trajekt
minibus	combi	minibus
taxi	taksi	taksi
ticket	biletë	karta
train	tren	voz
train station	stacioni i trenit	željeznička stanica

Hiking

English	Albanian	Montenegrin
cave	shpellë	špilja/pećina
forest	pyll	šuma
hill	kodër	brdo
lake	liqen	jezero
map	hartë	karta
meadow/pasture	livadh	livada
mountain	mal	planina
mountain hut	kasolle	planinarski dom
pass	qafë	prijevoj, sedlo
path	shteg	staza/planinarska staza
peak	majë	vrh, kuk
ridge	kreshtë	greben, hrbat, kukovi
road	rrugë	cesta

English	Albanian	Montenegrin
road (4WD)	udhë	bijela cesta
rock/rocky	gur/shkëmbor	kamen/kamenit
slippery	rrëshqitës	klizavo
steep	rrëpirë	strm
summit	majë	vrh, kuk
river	lumë	rijeka
shelter	kasolle	sklonište, bivak
spring	burim	izvor
stream	përrua	potok
tree	pemë	drvo
valley	luginë	dolina
water	ujë	voda
waterfall	ujëvarë	vodopad

Directions

English	Albanian	Montenegrin
Where is...?	Ku është...?	Gdje je...?
How far is...?	Sar larg...?	Koliko je daleko...?
Is it marked?	A është e sinjalizuar?	Je li markiran?
up	lart	gore
down	poshtë	dole
here	këtu	tu
there	atje	tamo
(on the) left	majtas	(na) lijevo
(on the) right	djathtas	(na) desno
straight ahead	drejt	ravno

Weather

English	Albanian	Montenegrin
cloudy	*vranët*	*oblačno*
cold	*ftohtë*	*hladno*
fog	*mjegull*	*magla*
hot	*nxehtë*	*vruće*
ice	*akull*	*led*
lightning	*vetëtimë*	*munja*
nightfall	*mugëtirë*	*pada mrak*
rain	*shi*	*kiša*
snow	*bore*	*snijeg*
sun	*me diell*	*sunce*
thunderstorm	*stuhi*	*oluja*
weather	*mot*	*vrijeme*
windy	*me errë*	*duva vjetar*

Numerals

English	Albanian	Montenegrin
0	*zero*	*nula*
1	*një*	*jedan*
2	*dy*	*dva*
3	*tre*	*tri*
4	*katër*	*četiri*
5	*pesë*	*pet*
6	*gjashtë*	*šest*
7	*shtatë*	*sedam*
8	*tetë*	*osam*
9	*nëntë*	*devet*
10	*dhjetë*	*deset*
100	*njëqind*	*sto*

Dangers and emergencies

English	Albanian	Montenegrin
ambulance	*ambulancë*	*hitna pomoć*
A&E	*urgjenca*	*hitna*
Danger!	*Rrezik!*	*Pazite!*
danger	*ous i rrezikshëm*	*opasno*
doctor	*doktor*	*doktor*
embassy	*ambasada*	*ambasada*
emergency	*urgjenca*	*hitna*
Help!	*Ndihmë!*	*U pomoć!*
hospital	*spitali*	*bolnica*
I'm lost	*Kam humbur rrugën*	*Izgubljen sam (m) / Izgubljena sam (f)*
injured	*plagosur*	*povređen*
landmines	*minuar*	*mine*
police	*polici*	*policija*

Common signs (including place names) in Cyrillic

Cyrillic	Roman alphabet	English
АУТОБУСКА СТАНИЦА	*autobuska stanica*	bus station
БОЛНИЦА	*bolnica*	hospital
ДОМ	*dom*	hut
ИЗВОР	*izvor*	spring
КАФАНА	*kafana*	café
КОСОВО	Kosovo	Kosovo
ОДЛАСЦИ	*odlasci*	departures
ПЕЋ	Peć (Pejë)	Peć (Pejë)
ПЛАВ	Plav	Plav

Cyrillic	Roman alphabet	English
ПОДГОРИЦА	Podgorica	Podgorica
ПРОКЛЕТИЈЕ	Prokletije	Prokletije
ПЕРОН	*peron*	platform
ПОЛАСЦИ	*polasci*	arrivals
ПОЛИЦЈА	*policija*	police
ПАЗИТЕ	*pazite*	danger, be careful
ПРИВАТНО	*privatno*	private
СКЛОНИШТЕ	*sklonište*	shelter
ВРХ	*vrh*	peak
ВОДА	*voda*	water

APPENDIX E
History timeline

c5700–4500BC – Vinča Neolithic culture widespread across the central Balkans.

Eighth–third century BC – Various Illyrian tribes established on the eastern Adriatic seaboard and further inland (including the Albanoi and the Taulantii in modern Albania, and the Autariatae in the area north of Prokletije), becoming increasingly powerful by the fourth century BC.

Seventh–sixth century BC – Corinthian colonists found cities along the Adriatic coast, including Antibaris (Bar) and Epidamnus (Durrës).

Fourth century BC – Celtic tribes settle along the middle Danube and expand southwards.

Third century BC – An Illyrian tribe, the Ardiaei, build a powerful kingdom on the Adriatic, which brings them into contact with the Romans.

229BC – Beginning of Roman conquest of Illyria.

Sixth century AD – Arrival of the Slavs in the Balkans.

c850 – Serbian tribes of Raška (near Novi Pazar in southern Serbia) unite against Bulgarian Empire.

c960 – Disintegration of Raška, expansion of Duklja (Roman Dioclea, near modern Podgorica).

1040 – Duklja becomes independent from Byzantium.

1077 – Mihajlo Vojislav, Serbian ruler of Duklja, receives royal crown from Pope Gregory VII.

12th century – Duklja incorporated into Raška (medieval Serbia); the name Duklja is gradually replaced by Zeta.

c1190 – Arbanon established as a semi-autonomous principality of the Byzantine Empire, in central Albania.

1204 – Fourth Crusade. The Republic of Venice seizes control of much of Albania, with Byzantium later retaking control of part of the south where they established the Despotate of Epirus.

1258 – The Angevin Kingdom of Sicily takes control of a large part of Albania.

1343–7 – Stephen Uroš IV Dušan ('The Mighty') of Serbia invades Albania.

1345 – After enlarging the medieval Serbian Empire to cover a vast area of the Balkans, Stefan Dušan proclaims himself 'Tsar of the Serbs and Romans'. Prizren becomes capital of the Serbian Empire, and the Serbian Archbishopric was raised to a Patriarchate, with its seat at Monastery of the Patriarchate of Peć (Pejë) in Kosovo.

1368 – Karl Thopia, an Albanian feudal prince, captures Durrës from the Angevins. Later, Thopia invites the Ottomans to support him against his Serbian rival, Balša II.

1389 – Ottoman defeat of Serbian and other Christian armies at the Battle of Kosovo (Kosovo polje), near modern Pristina, on 15 June.

1405 – Birth of George Kastrioti (later Skanderbeg), an Albanian nobleman who served the Ottomans until 1443.

1420 – Venetian conquest of the southern Adriatic coast.

1443 – Skanderbeg deserts the Ottomans at the Battle of Niš, enters Albania and reembraces Roman Catholicism.

1444 – Skenderbeg establishes the League of Lezhë with other Albanian noble families against the Ottomans. Defeat of numerically superior Ottoman forces by Skanderbeg at the battle of Torvioll.

1447–8 – Albanian Venetian War. Venice offers rewards for Skanderbeg's assassination, and invites the Ottomans to attack his forces simultaneously. Venetian forces routed by Skanderbeg and peace treaty signed.

1468 – Death of Skanderbeg.

1479 – Shkodër falls to the Ottomans.

Late 15th century– The Crnojević dynasty rules Zeta from Cetinje.

1480s – Ivan Crnojević accepts Ottoman suzerainty.

1516 – Election of first Vladika from the monastery at Cetinje.

1696 – Danilo I Petrović-Njegoš makes the position of Vladika hereditary rather than elective.

1700s – Widespread conversion of many Albanians to Islam.

1789 – Formal Ottoman recognition of Montenegro.

1797– Republic of Venice extinguished by Napoleon.

1830 – 500 Albanian leaders captured and killed after accepting an invitation to meet with an Ottoman general in Monastir.

1852 – Danilo II Petrović-Njegoš removes the requirement that a Vladika remain celibate, and gains permission to name his own heir.

1878 – Treaty of Berlin.

1905 – First Montenegrin constitution.

1910 – Montenegro proclaimed a constitutional monarchy.

1912 – The Balkan League (an alliance between Greece, Bulgaria, Serbia and Montenegro) attacks the Ottomans during the First Balkan War. Albania declares independence.

1913 – The London Peace Conference, convened by the Great Powers following the Balkan League victories over the Ottomans to arbitrate over territorial gains (the Balkan

League powers had intended to divide Albania among themselves), grants a large part of Albania to Serbia and Greece at the Treaty of London. Second Balkan War. Wilhelm of Wied of Germany installed as Prince of Albania by Great Powers, ignoring the provisional government already set up at Vlorë by delegates from across Albania.

1914 – Outbreak of WW1. Montenegro invades Albania. By 1915 Montenegro occupied by Austro-German forces.

1918 – Podgorica Assembly – King Nikola is deposed; Montenegro declared part of Serbia. Establishment of the Kingdom of Serbs, Croats and Slovenes, later known as Kingdom of Yugoslavia.

1919 – Paris Peace Conference – Albania divided between Greece, Italy and Kingdom of Yugoslavia.

1922 – Ahmet Zogu becomes Prime Minister in Albania.

1928 – Zogu crowns himself Zog I, King of the Albanians.

1933 – The Kanuni i Lekë Dukagjinit – an ancient set of tribal laws in northern Albania based on the pillars of honour, loyalty, good conduct and hospitality, and including laws on blood feud – is collected and published for the first time, by Shtjefën Gjeçovi, an Albanian Catholic priest and folklorist (it was previously passed down through generations orally).

1939 – Mussolini invades Albania, King Zog is forced to flee to Greece.

1941 – Hitler invades Kingdom of Yugoslavia.

1941 – Enver Hoxha becomes head of new Communist Party in Albania.

1943 – Capitulation of Italy; German invasion of Albania.

1944 – German withdrawal from Albania; Hoxha becomes new ruler of Albania.

1945 – Formation of Socialist Federal Republic of Yugoslavia, formed of six republics: Serbia, Croatia, Bosnia, Slovenia, Macedonia and Macedonia. Kosovo becomes an autonomous province within Serbia.

1946 – In Albania, purges of non-Communists from government positions.

1948 – Albania breaks ties with neighbouring Yugoslavia, and begins receiving economic aid from the Soviet Union.

1961 – Death of Zog I in Paris. Albania allies itself with China.

1967 – Albania declared the world's first atheist state.

1967–86 – Hoxha carries out policy of 'bunkerisation', building some half a million military bunkers in almost every conceivable location all over Albania.

1974 – The Socialist Autonomous Province of Kosovo gains increased autonomy within the Republic of Serbia.

1979 – Major earthquake off the Montenegrin coast.

1980 – Death of Tito.

1985 – Death of Hoxha.

1989 – Collapse of Communist rule in Eastern Europe. Serbian leader Slobodan Milošević reduces Kosovo's autonomous status within Serbia, and gives his infamous speech at the Gazimestan monument in Kosovo on the 600th anniversary of the Battle of Kosovo. Foundation of political party the Democratic League of Kosovo (LDK).

1990 – The Communist regime in Albania allows the formation of independent political parties in Albania. The Democratic Party of Albania (DP) is formed the following day.

1991 – Croatia and Slovenia declare independence from Yugoslavia; beginning of Croatian War of Independence; Montenegro supports Serbia, and joins the JNA in siege of Dubrovnik.

1991 – Multi-party elections in Albania won by the Communist Party.

1992 – In a referendum, Montenegrins vote by a 95% majority to remain with Serbia as part of Yugoslavia. In Kosovo, the Republic of Kosovo is proclaimed, with Ibrahim Rugova as its first President.

1993 – Formation of KLA (Kosovo Liberation Army).

1997 – Violent anti-government protests and rioting in Albania following the collapse of fraudulent pyramid investment schemes, and the loss of many people's life's savings. Up to one million weapons are looted during the unrest.

1999 – War in Kosovo between Serb forces and the KLA, supported by Nato airstrikes on Serbia, in the wake of attacks on Serbs by the KLA and mass killings of Albanians by Serb security forces. The Nato airstrikes also result in many civilian casualties. Mass influx of refugees from Kosovo cross the border into Albania. Following the war, the United Nations Interim Administration Mission in Kosovo (UNMIK) is established by the UN, and Kosovo Force (KFOR) is deployment by Nato, its aim to deter renewed hostility against Kosovo by Serb forces, and to demilitarise the KLA. In 2016, there were still 4600 KFOR troops in Kosovo.

2000 – Elections held in Kosovo.

2002 – Serbia and Montenegro, as the remaining portion of Yugoslavia, rename their union the State Union of Serbia and Montenegro.

2003 – Filip Vujanović elected President of Montenegro in 2003.

2004 – Four Serbian Orthodox churches and monasteries in Kosovo (Patriarchate of Peć Monastery, Dečani Monastery, Gračanica Monastery and the Church of Our Lady of Ljeviš in Prizren) are declared a UNESCO World Heritage Site, under the title Medieval Monuments in Kosovo.

2005 – Elections in Albania, with the Democratic Party of Albania emerging as the leading party in the new coalition government.

2006 – Montenegro holds referendum and votes by 55% majority for independence from Serbia.

2008 – Kosovo declares independence from Serbia; the declaration is recognised by most EU states as well as by Montenegro, but not by Serbia. As a result Kosovo's border with Montenegro remains disputed, with a 7km stretch of neutral territory running the length of the border between the two countries.

2009 – Albania joins Nato, and submits application for EU membership.

2010 – Montenegro attains formal candidacy for EU membership; Albania's bid for candidacy status is rejected.

2011 – North Kosovo Crisis – clashes between ethnic Serbs and Kosovo Police when the latter crossed into Serb-controlled areas in northern Kosovo, in an attempt to take control several border crossings without the prior consultation of either Serbia or KFOR.

2012 – Repatriation of King Zog's remains from Paris to Albania.

2012 – Milo Đukanović of the Democratic Party of Socialists of Montenegro, elected for his fourth non-consecutive term as Premier of Montenegro.

2013 – Edi Rama of Socialist party of Albania is elected Prime Minister in Albania.

2015 – Montenegro invited to join Nato. Isa Mustafa, leader of the Democratic League of Kosovo, elected Prime Minister in Kosovo.

2016 – EU recommends that Kosovo should be transferred to the visa-free list for short stays in the Schengen zone, on condition it moves forward towards ratifying a border demarcation agreement with Montenegro. There are opposition protests against the border deal, who say it deprives Kosovo of large areas of territory.

2017 – Elections held in both Kosovo and Albania with the Democratic Party of Kosovo taking the most seats in the former, though not with enough to form a government, and Edi Rama's Socialist Party winning a clear majority in the latter.

2018 – Kosovo's parliament ratifies the border demarcation line with Montenegro.

NOTES

NOTES

NOTES

LISTING OF CICERONE GUIDES

BRITISH ISLES CHALLENGES, COLLECTIONS AND ACTIVITIES

Cycling Land's End to John o' Groats
Great Walks on the England Coast Path
The Big Rounds
The Book of the Bivvy
The Book of the Bothy
The Mountains of England & Wales:
Vol 1 Wales
Vol 2 England
The National Trails
Walking the End to End Trail

SHORT WALKS SERIES

Short Walks Hadrian's Wall
Short Walks in Arnside and Silverdale
Short Walks in Dumfries and Galloway
Short Walks in Nidderdale
Short Walks in the Lake District: Windermere Ambleside and Grasmere
Short Walks in the Surrey Hills
Short Walks Lake District – Coniston and Langdale
Short Walks on the Malvern Hills
Short Walks Winchester

SCOTLAND

Ben Nevis and Glen Coe
Cycle Touring in Northern Scotland
Cycling in the Hebrides
Cycling the North Coast 500
Great Mountain Days in Scotland
Mountain Biking in Southern and Central Scotland
Mountain Biking in West and North West Scotland
Not the West Highland Way
Scotland
Scotland's Best Small Mountains
Scotland's Mountain Ridges
Scottish Wild Country Backpacking
Skye's Cuillin Ridge Traverse
The Borders Abbeys Way
The Great Glen Way
The Great Glen Way Map Booklet
The Hebridean Way
The Hebrides
The Isle of Mull
The Isle of Skye
The Skye Trail
The Southern Upland Way
The West Highland Way
The West Highland Way Map Booklet
Walking Ben Lawers, Rannoch and Atholl
Walking in the Cairngorms

Walking in the Pentland Hills
Walking in the Scottish Borders
Walking in the Southern Uplands
Walking in Torridon, Fisherfield, Fannichs and An Teallach
Walking Loch Lomond and the Trossachs
Walking on Arran
Walking on Harris and Lewis
Walking on Jura, Islay and Colonsay
Walking on Rum and the Small Isles
Walking on the Orkney and Shetland Isles
Walking on Uist and Barra
Walking the Cape Wrath Trail
Walking the Corbetts
Vol 1 South of the Great Glen
Vol 2 North of the Great Glen
Walking the Galloway Hills
Walking the John o' Groats Trail
Walking the Munros
Vol 1 – Southern, Central and Western Highlands
Vol 2 – Northern Highlands and the Cairngorms
Winter Climbs in the Cairngorms
Winter Climbs: Ben Nevis and Glen Coe

NORTHERN ENGLAND ROUTES

Cycling the Reivers Route
Cycling the Way of the Roses
Hadrian's Cycleway
Hadrian's Wall Path
Hadrian's Wall Path Map Booklet
The Coast to Coast Cycle Route
The Coast to Coast Walk
The Coast to Coast Walk Map Booklet
The Pennine Way
The Pennine Way Map Booklet
Walking the Dales Way
Walking the Dales Way Map Booklet

NORTH-EAST ENGLAND, YORKSHIRE DALES AND PENNINES

Cycling in the Yorkshire Dales
Great Mountain Days in the Pennines
Mountain Biking in the Yorkshire Dales
The Cleveland Way and the Yorkshire Wolds Way
The Cleveland Way Map Booklet
The North York Moors
Trail and Fell Running in the Yorkshire Dales
Walking in County Durham
Walking in Northumberland
Walking in the North Pennines

Walking in the Yorkshire Dales: North and East
Walking in the Yorkshire Dales: South and West
Walking St Cuthbert's Way
Walking St Oswald's Way and Northumberland Coast Path

NORTH-WEST ENGLAND AND THE ISLE OF MAN

Cycling the Pennine Bridleway
Isle of Man Coastal Path
The Lancashire Cycleway
The Lune Valley and Howgills
Walking in Cumbria's Eden Valley
Walking in Lancashire
Walking in the Forest of Bowland and Pendle
Walking on the Isle of Man
Walking on the West Pennine Moors
Walking the Ribble Way
Walks in Silverdale and Arnside

LAKE DISTRICT

Bikepacking in the Lake District
Cycling in the Lake District
Great Mountain Days in the Lake District
Joss Naylor's Lakes, Meres and Waters of the Lake District
Lake District Winter Climbs
Lake District: High Level and Fell Walks
Lake District: Low Level and Lake Walks
Mountain Biking in the Lake District
Outdoor Adventures with Children – Lake District
Scrambles in the Lake District – North
Scrambles in the Lake District – South
Trail and Fell Running in the Lake District
Walking The Cumbria Way
Walking the Lake District Fells:
Borrowdale
Buttermere
Coniston
Keswick
Langdale
Mardale and the Far East
Patterdale
Wasdale
Walking the Tour of the Lake District

DERBYSHIRE, PEAK DISTRICT AND MIDLANDS

Cycling in the Peak District
Dark Peak Walks
Scrambles in the Dark Peak
Walking in Derbyshire

Walking in the Peak District –
   White Peak East
Walking in the Peak District –
   White Peak West

SOUTHERN ENGLAND

20 Classic Sportive Rides:
   In South East England
   In South West England
Cycling in the Cotswolds
Mountain Biking on the
   North Downs
Mountain Biking on the
   South Downs
Suffolk Coast and Heath Walks
The Cotswold Way
The Cotswold Way Map Booklet
The Kennet and Avon Canal
The Lea Valley Walk
The North Downs Way
The North Downs Way Map Booklet
The Peddars Way and Norfolk
   Coast Path
The Pilgrims' Way
The Ridgeway National Trail
The Ridgeway National Trail
   Map Booklet
The South Downs Way
The South Downs Way Map Booklet
The Thames Path
The Thames Path Map Booklet
The Two Moors Way
Two Moors Way Map Booklet
Walking Hampshire's Test Way
Walking in Cornwall
Walking in Essex
Walking in Kent
Walking in London
Walking in Norfolk
Walking in the Chilterns
Walking in the Cotswolds
Walking in the Isles of Scilly
Walking in the New Forest
Walking in the North Wessex Downs
Walking on Dartmoor
Walking on Guernsey
Walking on Jersey
Walking on the Isle of Wight
Walking the Dartmoor Way
Walking the Jurassic Coast
Walking the South West Coast Path
Walking the South West Coast Path
   Map Booklets:
   Vol 1: Minehead to St Ives
   Vol 2: St Ives to Plymouth
   Vol 3: Plymouth to Poole
Walks in the South Downs
   National Park

WALES AND WELSH BORDERS

Cycle Touring in Wales
Cycling Lon Las Cymru
Great Mountain Days in Snowdonia

Hillwalking in Shropshire
Mountain Walking in Snowdonia
Offa's Dyke Path
Offa's Dyke Path Map Booklet
Ridges of Snowdonia
Scrambles in Snowdonia
Snowdonia –
   30 Low-level and Easy Walks:
   – North
   – South
The Cambrian Way
The Pembrokeshire Coast Path
The Snowdonia Way
The Wye Valley Walk
Walking in Carmarthenshire
Walking in Pembrokeshire
Walking in the Brecon Beacons
Walking in the Forest of Dean
Walking in the Wye Valley
Walking on Gower
Walking the Severn Way
Walking the Shropshire Way
Walking the Wales Coast Path

**INTERNATIONAL CHALLENGES,
COLLECTIONS AND ACTIVITIES**

Europe's High Points
Walking the Via Francigena
   Pilgrim Route – Part 1

AFRICA

Kilimanjaro
Walking in the Drakensberg
Walks and Scrambles in the
   Moroccan Anti-Atlas

ALPS CROSS-BORDER ROUTES

100 Hut Walks in the Alps
Alpine Ski Mountaineering
   Vol 1 – Western Alps
The Karnischer Hohenweg
The Tour of the Bernina
Trail Running – Chamonix and the
   Mont Blanc region
Trekking Chamonix to Zermatt
Trekking in the Alps
Trekking in the Silvretta and
   Ratikon Alps
Trekking Munich to Venice
Trekking the Tour of Mont Blanc
Walking in the Alps

**PYRENEES AND FRANCE/SPAIN
CROSS-BORDER ROUTES**

Shorter Treks in the Pyrenees
The GR11 Trail
The Pyrenean Haute Route
The Pyrenees
Walks and Climbs in the Pyrenees

AUSTRIA

Innsbruck Mountain Adventures
Trekking Austria's Adlerweg

Trekking in Austria's Hohe Tauern
Trekking in Austria's Zillertal Alps
Trekking in the Stubai Alps
Walking in Austria
Walking in the Salzkammergut:
   the Austrian Lake District

EASTERN EUROPE

The Danube Cycleway Vol 2
The Elbe Cycle Route
The High Tatras
The Mountains of Romania
Walking in Hungary

**FRANCE, BELGIUM
AND LUXEMBOURG**

Camino de Santiago – Via Podiensis
Chamonix Mountain Adventures
Cycle Touring in France
Cycling London to Paris
Cycling the Canal de la Garonne
Cycling the Canal du Midi
Cycling the Route des Grandes Alpes
Mont Blanc Walks
Mountain Adventures in
   the Maurienne
Short Treks on Corsica
The GR5 Trail
The GR5 Trail – Benelux
   and Lorraine
The GR5 Trail – Vosges and Jura
The Grand Traverse of the
   Massif Central
The Moselle Cycle Route
The River Loire Cycle Route
The River Rhone Cycle Route
Trekking in the Vanoise
Trekking the Cathar Way
Trekking the GR10
Trekking the GR20 Corsica
Trekking the Robert Louis
   Stevenson Trail
Via Ferratas of the French Alps
Walking in Provence – East
Walking in Provence – West
Walking in the Ardennes
Walking in the Auvergne
Walking in the Briançonnais
Walking in the Dordogne
Walking in the Haute Savoie: North
Walking in the Haute Savoie: South
Walking on Corsica
Walking the Brittany Coast Path

GERMANY

Hiking and Cycling in the
   Black Forest
The Danube Cycleway Vol 1
The Rhine Cycle Route
The Westweg
Walking in the Bavarian Alps